*Embracing
Judaism*

# Embracing Judaism

SIMCHA KLING

---

THE RABBINICAL ASSEMBLY
*New York*

ACKNOWLEDGMENTS

Excerpt from *The Sabbath* by Abraham Joshua Heschel, copyright © 1951 by Abraham Joshua Heschel. Copyright renewed 1979 by Sylvia Heschel. Reprinted by permission of Farrar, Straus and Giroux, Inc.

Excerpt from *God in Search of Man* by Abraham Joshua Heschel, copyright © 1955 by Abraham Joshua Heschel. Reprinted by permission of Farrar, Straus and Giroux, Inc.

*Cover:* From the opening page of *Pirkei Avot,* folio 139 in the Rothschild Mahzor, Florence, 1492. Courtesy of the Library of the Jewish Theological Seminary of America.

Library of Congress Catalog Card Number: 86-63681
International Standard Book Number: 0-916219-02-x

10 9 8 7 6 5 4 3 2 1

MANUFACTURED IN THE UNITED STATES OF AMERICA
DESIGNED BY BETTY BINNS GRAPHICS/BETTY BINNS

# Contents

PREFACE, vii
INTRODUCTION, ix

| | | |
|---|---|---|
| 1 | *Jews by Choice: Then and Now* | 1 |
| 2 | *What Does Judaism Teach?* | 11 |
| 3 | *Religious Movements in Judaism* | 27 |
| 4 | *How Do Jews Worship?* | 36 |
| 5 | *Holy Days and Festivals* | 62 |
| 6 | *Judaism: A Way of Living* | 75 |
| 7 | *The Jewish Life Cycle* | 90 |
| 8 | *History: Ancient and Medieval* | 102 |

v

9  *History: Modern Times*                         122

10  *American Jewish History*                       141

11  *Zionism and the State of Israel*               151

12  *Judaism and Christianity*                      162

13  *A Personal Story of Conversion,*              174
    BY RACHEL COWAN

    CLOSING WORDS, 183
    INDEX, 185

# *Preface*

*T*HIS book is an introduction and guide to the vast panorama of Jewish religious civilization. Its preparation demanded a great deal of labor, love, knowledge, skill, and patience of those who helped in evaluating, editing, and rewriting my manuscript and in seeing it through the press. I am both grateful and indebted to those who have shared in the labors. My colleague and classmate Rabbi Simon Glustrom, who serves on the Rabbinical Assembly Publications Committee, has reviewed every sentence, both before and after editing, and has made valuable suggestions. The exceptionally capable Rachel Cowan and Nancy Wingerson reacted to the original manuscript and have contributed to its clarification and readability. Rachel Cowan helped with revisions and contributed her own chapter. My friend Rabbi Jules Harlow, who is responsible for all publications of the Rabbinical Assembly, deserves thanks for his constant and most appreciated advice and editorial skills. His translations of passages from the prayerbook (as in *Siddur Sim Shalom*) and from the Mishnah and Maimonides (as in *Maḥzor for Rosh Hashanah and Yom Kippur*) are used throughout this volume. They appear as unattributed indented matter and are reprinted by permission of the Rabbinical Assembly. My wife, Edith Leeman Kling, has always inspired, assisted, and encouraged me, enabling me to work, for which I have always been grateful.

SIMCHA KLING
*Louisville, Kentucky*

# Introduction

*I*F you are thinking about conversion to Judaism, you probably have many questions. What does converting mean? What
is expected of me? Who will help me? What am I supposed to
believe? What do Jews think about converts? Will I ever feel
Jewish? Most people ask these and many other questions during
the months or years that they spend making the decision to convert.

This book will answer some of your questions about the
conversion process. Technically, the procedure is straightforward. Emotionally, however, it may be more difficult. Potential
converts have to work out their own complicated family relationships while confronting attitudes in the Jewish community
that may at first be baffling to them.

This book begins by discussing the history of conversion to
Judaism, and Jewish attitudes about conversion. It also includes
a convert's description of her own conversion process, in which
she highlights some of the emotional issues which are involved.
The book, however, is more than a discussion of conversion. It

is a comprehensive introduction to Judaism, presenting the basics of Jewish tradition, ritual, theology, worship, and history. It will also acquaint you with some of the most important issues that concern the Jewish community today.

Each chapter of the book presents information and ideas that call for further exploration. The bibliography at the end of each chapter suggests further readings. One of the wondrous aspects of Judaism is that it provides such a vast and rich literature to study. Everyone, regardless of background, can find new meanings and new understanding with each reading of the Torah, of other biblical texts and commentaries, or of postbiblical literature from every era. Many Jews believe that revelation did not end when God gave the Torah to Moses on Mount Sinai. Revelation is a continuing process that unfolds at each confrontation with a Jewish text.

In the words of Dr. Abraham Joshua Heschel, "Revelation is not vicarious thinking. Its purpose is not to substitute for but to extend our understanding. . . . We must look for ways of translating biblical commandments into programs required by our own conditions. The full meaning of the biblical words was not disclosed once and for all. The word was given once; the effort to understand it must go on forever."

An ancient story tells of a non-Jew's visit to Shammai, the great teacher of the first pre-Christian century. "Teach me the whole Torah while I stand on one foot," said the non-Jew. "Then I will convert." Shammai, renowned for his short temper, was enraged by the man's mockery and drove him away. The non-Jew then went to Shammai's colleague, the gentle Hillel, to repeat the challenge. Hillel responded patiently, " 'Do not unto others what you would not have them do to you.' The rest is commentary. Now go and learn."

This book presents Judaism as a whole "on one foot." The rest waits for you to explore through study and experience during the rest of your life. Go and learn!

## *Suggested Readings for Further Study*

Gordis, Robert, *The Root and the Branch* (Chicago: University of Chicago Press, 1962)

Kertzer, Morris, *What Is a Jew?* (New York: World Publishing Co., 1960)

Steinberg, Milton, *Basic Judaism* (New York: Harcourt, Brace Jovanovitch, 1947)

ADDITIONAL SUGGESTIONS

De Sola Pool, David, *Why I am a Jew* (New York: Bloch Publishing Co., 1957)

Dresner, Samuel, and Sherwin, Byron, *Judaism* (New York: United Synagogue, 1978)

Finkelstein, Louis, editor, *The Jews: Their History, Culture and Religion* (Philadelphia: The Jewish Publication Society, 1949)

Gittlesohn, Roland, *The Modern Meaning of Judaism* (Cleveland and New York: Collins, 1978)

*Jewish Values* (Jerusalem: Keter Publishing House, 1974)

Millgram, Abraham E., *Concepts That Distinguish Judaism* (Washington, D.C.: B'nai B'rith Books, 1985)

Strassfeld, Sharon, and Strassfeld, Michael, *The Third Jewish Catalog* (Philadelphia: Jewish Publication Society, 1980)

Wouk, Herman, *This Is My God* (Garden City, New York: Doubleday and Company, 1961)

*Embracing
Judaism*

# CHAPTER I

# *Jews by Choice: Then and Now*

*T*HE number of people choosing to become Jewish in the United States today is unprecedented in modern history. As a result of this phenomenon, American Judaism is becoming more open to Jews by choice. Many Jews, however, still maintain the erroneous belief that converts are not really Jewish, a position which may begin with their pride in the fact that Judaism does not proselytize. Such Jews might be more comfortable with the whole topic if they studied the history of conversion to Judaism. They would find that there have been periods in Jewish history when proselytism was encouraged. Today's residual reluctance to accept converts comes from a fairly recent period of Jewish history. It will change as more people come to value the contribution that Jews by choice are making to Jewish life.

During the biblical period, prior to the destruction of the Temple in Jerusalem in 586 B.C.E.,* the concept of conversion did

---

*B.C.E. is the abbreviated form of "Before the Common Era," i.e., before Christianity. Jews use it rather than B.C. ("Before Christ") since the word "Christ" means "Messiah" and Jews do not accept Jesus as Messiah.

not exist. When Israelite men married non-Israelite women, they expected their wives to leave their idols at home and worship the God of the Israelites. The wives became members of the tribe. When Israelite women married non-Israelite men, they joined their husbands' tribes. The Torah proscribes only marriage to Canaanite women. The Bible records mixed marriage; Moses, David, and Solomon married non-Israelite women. Boaz married a Moabite woman; the story of their marriage is portrayed in the biblical book which bears her name: Ruth.

The Hebrew word for convert is *ger* (plural: *gerim*). The literal meaning of *ger* in biblical days was "resident alien," a non-Israelite who lived in the land of Israel and was respectful of God, but who owned no land and had no political rights. The Torah is filled with admonitions to the Israelites to treat the *gerim* well, for we were once *gerim* (also translated as strangers) in Egypt and we remember our suffering there.

The first conversions occurred during the Babylonian Exile (which began in the sixth century B.C.E.). Many people were attracted to the Jewish religion and became part of the Jewish people, even though they did not live in the land of Israel. The prophet Isaiah referred to them as "those who joined themselves to the Lord" (Isaiah 56:3–7), and promised them that they would be part of the return to Zion.

After the return and the rebuilding of the Temple in Jerusalem (in the late sixth and early fifth centuries), Jews engaged in extensive proselytization. Even Roman nobility converted to Judaism. So did Queen Helena of Adiabene and her entire royal family. The ancient rabbis formulated laws of conversion which still remain in effect in almost the same form. The established procedure began by asking the prospective convert if he or she understood the suffering with which the Jewish people have been afflicted continually. The prospective proselyte who still wanted to become Jewish was taught the laws, major and minor alike. A person who came "under the wings of the Divine Presence" reenacted the people Israel's entry into the Divine Covenant with God. The ritual of conversion included circumcision for men and ritual immersion in water *(tevilah)* and the offering of a sacrifice for men and women alike. The formal proceedings which followed included a statement of commitment and had to be witnessed by a religious court *(bet din)* of three men. The only requirement that has been changed by traditional Judaism is the elimination of sacrifice.

The Talmud contains many discussions about conversions and converts. One major issue is whether converts may recite certain phrases, such as "God of our fathers" or "God who has chosen us." Some rabbis maintained that converts may not recite these words because their natural ancestors had not been chosen by God, and did not worship Him. Other rabbinic authorities argued that proselytes may recite the phrases as descendants of Abraham, their spiritual ancestor, and this has remained the dominant view in Jewish tradition.

Most rabbis believed that "when a proselyte comes to be converted, one receives him with an open hand to bring him under the wings of the Divine Presence." Authorities by and large refused to generalize from the few bad experiences they had encountered with proselytes. According to tradition, several great rabbis, including Rabbi Meir and Rabbi Akiba, were descended from converts.

In the sixth and seventh centuries, after the close of the Talmudic period, conversion became a capital offense for both Christians and Jews, according to the law of the land. Nevertheless, Christians, especially those who lived in Muslim countries where conversion was not illegal, continued to choose Judaism. Other non-Jews converted in large numbers. The fifth-century kings of Himyar (in southern Arabia) and the eighth-century rulers of Khazaria and their subjects converted to Judaism.

In later years a steady trickle of people became proselytes. Some Christian clergymen, after studying what they called the Old Testament, came to feel that they would rather be Jewish. A priest named Vicilinus who lived in Mainz in 1012 wrote treatises on the inherent truth of Judaism. The Jews were soon expelled from Mainz, probably as a punishment for this man's writings.

Andreas, bishop of Bari, fled Italy after he was ritually circumcised and lived in the large Jewish community in Cairo. When a young Norman nobleman named Obadiah heard of his actions in 1100, he too left the priesthood and converted. He was jailed, but he managed to escape and flee to Baghdad. Thereafter he traveled throughout the Near East. His journal is preserved in a Cairo library.

Maimonides, the great medieval authority, while living in Cairo wrote responses to inquiries from Jews all over the world. He was concerned about proselytes; to one troubled soul he wrote:

> As every native Israelite prays and recites blessings . . . so anyone who becomes a proselyte throughout the generations and anyone who unifies the Name of the Holy One as it is written in the Torah is a pupil of our father Abraham, and all of them are members of his household. . . . hence you may say: "Our God, and God of our fathers," for Abraham, peace be upon him, is your father . . . Since you have come beneath the wings of the Divine Presence and attached yourself to Him, there is no difference between us and you. . . . You certainly may recite the blessings, "Who has chosen us, Who has given us, Who has caused us to inherit, and Who has separated us." For the Creator has already chosen you and has separated you from the nations and has given you the Torah, as the Torah was given to us and to proselytes. . . . Further, do not belittle your lineage; if we trace our descent to Abraham, Isaac, and Jacob, your connection is with Him by Whose word the universe came into being.

Writing to a proselyte who felt humiliated by the attitudes of other Jews toward him, Maimonides declared:

> Toward father and mother we are commanded honor and reverence, toward the prophets to obey them, but toward proselytes we are commanded to have great love in our inmost hearts. . . . God, in His glory, loves proselytes. . . . A man who left his father

and birthplace and the realm of his people at a time when they
were powerful, who understood with his insight, and who attached himself to this nation which today is a despised people,
the slaves of rulers, and recognized and knew that their religion is
true and righteous . . . and pursued God . . . and came beneath
the wings of the Divine Presence . . . the Lord does not call you
fool, but intelligent and understanding, wise and walking correctly, a pupil of our father Abraham.


When the First Crusade was launched in 1096, a proselyte
was among the Jews who were burned at the stake in England
when Christians attacked them in an early burst of zeal. People
continued to convert to Judaism throughout the Middle Ages,
even though the act was dangerous for both the proselyte and the
teacher. Some prominent Jewish scholars maintained even then
that the purpose of the dispersion of the Jews was to gain
proselytes.

By the end of the fifteenth century, the Jews had turned in-
ward. The gulf between them and the gentile world seemed un-
bridgeable. Rabbi Solomon Luria summed up the feeling in the
sixteenth century: "Would that the seed of Israel continue to stand
fast and hold its own among the nations throughout the days of
our exile and no stranger be added who is not of our nation."
Although rabbinic authorities had cooled to the idea of seeking
out converts, they would work with someone who insistently
sought them out.

When ideas of the Enlightenment became prominent in the
eighteenth century, Jews were allowed back into society's mainstream. This new acceptance, though, intensified the Jewish
community's reluctance to accept proselytes. The Jews came to
accept Christians as monotheists bound to God by the Covenant
that God had made with Noah. They no longer viewed them as
pagan idolators, so they no longer felt that Judaism was the only
way in which Christians could come "under the sheltering wings
of God." As religious tolerance became more widespread, Jews
became more convinced that they should not proselytize.

Modern Judaism continued to make a virtue of refusing to seek out converts. Only gradually has that attitude begun to change in the United States. The Reform movement took the lead in reaching out to potential converts. It simplified the conversion process, and it has urged Jews to reverse the usual stand against proselytizing. Because of their interpretation of Jewish tradition, Reform authorities are generally less demanding in their requirements for the religious rituals to be fulfilled. The Conservative movement also welcomes Jews by choice.

The attitudes of most Jews toward conversion differ greatly from the attitudes of most Christians. Christianity has always sought to preach to the unconverted throughout the world. Christian missionaries believe that they are performing a holy act when they convert people to Christianity, for they believe that they are saving the converts' souls, guaranteeing them eternal life in Heaven. Jews, on the other hand, do not maintain that their religion is the only true one. They believe that Judaism is the true religion for Jews but that the righteous of all peoples will receive the same rewards as righteous Jews. They would be content if all people who believe in one God would live faithfully by their own religious teachings.

Today many Jews care deeply about people who are seriously interested in choosing Judaism, and are anxious to help them. They explain to the newcomers that choosing to become Jewish is different from changing from one Christian denomination to another. A convert to Judaism not only adopts a new theology and different ritual practices and customs but also joins a different people. To be a Jew means belonging to a unique historical community. The community is neither racially nor genetically defined, since those born outside it may become fully accepted members. Yet it is a community in which history, culture, and tradition have been transmitted through family. Therefore, family is very important. People not born into the community need to learn its history, culture, and traditions.

It is sometimes difficult for a newcomer to understand what

Jewishness is. Paradoxically, it is easier for Jews to say what it is *not* than what it *is*. Judaism, of course, is a religion, but there are Jews who do not claim to be religious. Jews have many national characteristics—a relationship to a specific land (Israel), to specific languages (Hebrew and Yiddish), and to their literatures, and a historic memory of national independence and kinship—yet Jews are citizens of many nations. Whatever they feel about the State of Israel, they are loyal and active citizens of the countries where they live, at home in the languages and cultures of those countries.

Jews are best defined as a people (*am* in Hebrew), bearers of the Jewish religious civilization. Everyone who identifies as a member of the Jewish people is an heir to its teachings, beliefs, practices, and outlook. As the Orthodox and Conservative movements interpret Jewish law, the child of a Jewish mother is a Jew. If the mother is not Jewish, or if she converts after the child's birth, the child must convert in order to be considered Jewish.

Any person who goes through a traditional, rabbinically supervised process of conversion is a Jew. In 1983, the Reform rabbis decided that the child of one Jewish parent, either father or mother, is considered to be a Jew if raised as one by the parents.

The conversion process involves extensive study with a rabbi or other teacher for a length of time determined by the supervising rabbi. During this period, the students learn history, theology, rituals, traditions, and Hebrew. They read widely and have a chance to make sure that the teachings of Judaism are wholly acceptable to them and they do not still cherish beliefs that are incompatible with Judaism. They also learn about the history of anti-Semitism and must understand that they are choosing to join a people who have suffered intensely just because they were Jews.

When the students have completed their course of study and are deemed ready to convert, they proceed to the formal conversion ritual. Since conversion is a legal procedure in Jewish law, it must be done in the presence of a Jewish court *(bet din;* plural:

*batei din*). The specific acts of the *bet din* depend on the local rabbi. There are some *batei din* whose members ask the candidate questions to ascertain the individual's knowledge and sincerity. There are others who accept the word of the rabbi (or other instructor) and act solely as formal witnesses. It should be pointed out that in some matters of Jewish jurisprudence, a *bet din* must consist of ordained rabbis; in other matters, such as conversion, it may include observant Jewish laymen and does not require three ordained rabbis. The *bet din* may meet in the rabbi's study or in a small sanctuary. If the *bet din* does not pose questions to the candidate, it may simply assemble in the building that houses the small ritual bath called the *mikvah*.

The *mikvah* is a square tiled pool about five feet deep. It is filled with water in which the candidate immerses himself or herself. He or she wears nothing, removing even jewelry in order that nothing separate the water from the body. A Jewish witness (of the same sex as the convert) is present to be of help and to make sure that the immersion is ritually proper. After complete immersion the convert recites two blessings. The first praises God for the religious act of immersion:

> *Barukh atah Adonai, Eloheinu melekh ha-olam, asher kid'shanu b'mitzvotav v'tzivanu al ha-tevilah.*

> Praised Are You, Lord our God, King of the Universe whose mitzvot add holiness to our lives and who gave us the mitzvah of immersion.

The second blessing is one that is recited on many special occasions when people want to thank God for enabling them to experience that moment:

> *Barukh atah Adonai, Eloheinu melekh ha-olam, she-heh-khe-ya-nu v'keey'manu v'hee-gee-anu lazman hazeh.*

> Praised are You, Lord our God, King of the Universe who has kept us alive, preserved us and enabled us to reach this day.

If the convert is a boy or man, he will have to be circumcised before going to the *mikvah*. If he is already circumcised, he need only complete the ritual of circumcision by a procedure in which a drop of blood is drawn from the tip of the male organ. One who performs ritual circumcisions is called a *mohel,* an observant Jew who is carefully trained. In Jewish tradition, circumcision is not simply a medical procedure, nor is it a ritual performed for the sake of hygiene. It is a religious act, the marking of the sign of the convenant between God and the people Israel. The covenant was first marked in this manner when Abraham circumcised himself, his children, and his servants. Ever since then it has been solemnized in the same way.

Immersion in the *mikvah* is likewise a spiritual act. People sometimes mistakenly think its purpose is to rid a woman of uncleanness or to wash away a convert's previous life. Some people convey an attitude that the convert's former religious commitment reflected a lesser state of holiness, but the act of conversion should never be taken to imply a negative assessment of a former religion or of those who still adhere to it. Ritual immersion in the *mikvah* represents for all Jews, men and women, a symbolic rebirth into another level of spirituality, a new beginning.

Some people choose to bring a friend to the *mikvah*. Some choose to participate in a religious service after the ritual immersion or on the following Shabbat in order to celebrate publicly their becoming Jewish. Others choose to limit the participants in this process.

Once the ritual is completed, the converts are full-fledged Jews. They each choose a Hebrew name (it may be a translation of their English name, a name that begins with a similar sound, or an entirely different name). They will always be known by that name in religious rituals. Jews are never to speak of converts derogatorily or with condescension. Everyone must come to realize that it is wrong to think of a convert as someone who is not "really Jewish" and to refer to a marriage between a Jew by choice and a Jew by birth as an intermarriage. There is only one class of Jew in the family of the Jewish people.

Jews by choice have cast their lot with the God of Israel and the people Israel. They are deemed worthy descendants of Abraham and Sarah, Isaac and Rebecca, and Jacob, Leah, and Rachel, together with all other Jews.

## Suggested Readings for Further Study

Carmel, Abraham, *So Strange My Path* (New York: Bloch Publishing Company, 1964)

Cowan, Paul, *An Orphan in History* (Garden City, N.Y.: Doubleday, 1982)

ADDITIONAL SUGGESTIONS

Eichhorn, David Max, editor, *Conversion to Judaism: A History and Analysis* (New York: KTAV Publishing House, 1965)

Rosenbloom, Joseph R., *Conversion to Judaism: From the Biblical Period to the Present* (Cincinnati: Hebrew Union College Press, 1978)

Wigoder, Devorah, *Hope Is My House* (Englewood Cliffs, New Jersey: Prentice-Hall, 1966)

# CHAPTER 2

# What Does Judaism Teach?

*A* Jew is a person who was born into the Jewish people or a person who has chosen to become part of the Jewish people. A Jew is neither required nor expected to articulate a particular credo. At the moment of ordination, rabbis make no confession of faith; they are ordained because they have acquired enough knowledge to be recognized religious authorities. A young person upon becoming a Bar Mitzvah or a Bat Mitzvah does not vow allegiance to a formulated dogma but rather leads and/or participates in part of a synagogue service, thus demonstrating the ability to join the congregation as a regular participant.

Judaism, however, has always made affirmations, has always taken stands. Certain beliefs have been accepted by all religious Jews. There have been boundaries beyond which one could not go and still remain within the Jewish fold.

From time to time, authorities have attempted to set down what they felt to be the basic principles of Judaism. One of the

greatest rabbinic authorities of all time, Moses Maimonides of
twelfth-century Spain and Egypt, composed Thirteen Principles
of Faith. They were later adapted as a hymn which is widely used
in synagogue services *(Yigdal)*. Although these principles were
accepted for hundreds of years, they never became binding. Other
authorities disagreed with some of them. Succeeding writers tried
reducing them to five or to three principles, or even to one principle. Each effort remained the personal statement of one individual.

From its very beginnings, Judaism has contained strands of
different thoughts. Within the same general framework people
have viewed society and God from differing perspectives. The
authors of the Psalms did not look at God and mortals in the
same way that the authors of Judges, Job, or Ecclesiastes did. One
writer expressed his faith in a very simple manner, another in a
much more sophisticated way; one person emphasized the emotional, another the intellectual, aspect; one book was an out-
pouring of piety, another a philosophic inquiry.

The classic text of Jewish law, the third-century Mishnah,
records both majority and minority opinions of the ancient rabbis. The *Gemara,* the sixth-century collection of the rabbinic discussions which took place from the close of the Mishnah to the
year 499 of the Common Era, reflects the wide variety of the
theological understandings of the many great rabbis of those
years. The tradition of encouraging debate and diversity has remained essential to Jewish religious thinking ever since.

Though there always has been room for theological diversity within Judaism, there has been a strict definition of Jewish
conduct, a definite code establishing how an observant Jew should
live. Rabbis debated the interpretation of various details within
the system of law, called *halakhah,* but once they reached a decision, the ruling was binding. (At the same time, one must realize that there are differences of opinion on matters of Jewish law
as well. Different groups within the Jewish community often look
to their own specific authorities for interpretations on matters of

Jewish law.) Religious Jews, however they conceive of God, believe that it is necessary for Jews to pray together with others in the Jewish community, to observe the Sabbath in a special way, to eat in accordance with regulations of dietary laws *(kashrut),* and to fulfill additional commandments *(mitzvot).*

Judaism, a religion with its specific laws and with various conceptions of God, immortality, and the Messiah, embraces all types: mystics and rationalists, the unsophisticated and the highly educated, the followers of one sage and the disciples of another.

From these many strands of Jewish thought, one can weave some major teachings on basic theological issues. This book will discuss some of the most important, but you should refer to the suggested readings at the end of each chapter for the names of the books in which these ideas are discussed more fully and in much greater depth.

## Teachings on God

Every morning and evening the religious Jew at prayer recites the biblical verse which contains the essence of Jewish belief. No religious Jew would have any hesitation in affirming: *Sh'ma yisrael Adonai Eloheinu Adonai eḥad* ("Hear, O Israel: The Lord our God, the Lord is One"). This proclamation of pure monotheism insists that God is not plural and that God is not a divine being in human form. As Rabbi Louis Jacobs has pointed out, it is "a denial of polytheism. . . . Allied to this is the fact that God in His essence is indivisible. . . . Monotheism is not a mere mathematical reduction of gods until only one is left. . . . It teaches that the proper understanding of what 'God' means can only result in the belief that there *can* be only one God."

From its very inception, Judaism has never compromised on the oneness of God. There is only one God, and this one God is indivisible. Other ancient religions saw many powers at work in the universe, all of them in conflict with one another. The Bible taught that God is the unique Supreme Ruler who governs all and that the various deities that are worshiped simply do not exist. In ancient Persia, people believed in the religion of Zoroaster, which taught that two rival powers, Light and Darkness, continually struggle for supremacy. Judaism could not accept this dualism, for in Judaism God is the sole Master of all. As Christianity developed, it insisted that the one God was made up of three parts (the Trinity); Judaism considered this doctrine as diluted monotheism and rejected it.

Although Jews have always proclaimed God's oneness and uniqueness, they never defined God's nature precisely. They have believed that finite, mortal human beings can not define God, who is infinite and immortal. As Rabbi Saadiah Gaon of tenth-century Egypt said, "If I understood Him, I would be He."

Even Moses, who is depicted in the Torah as having come closer to God than any other human being, could not fully comprehend Him. Maimonides insisted that we can assert only what God is *not*. As formulated in the hymn *Yigdal* (based on his Thirteen Principles of Faith), "He is not a body, nor does He have the appearance of a body."

Despite Maimonides' doctrine of God's "negative attributes", there are some characteristics of God that can be asserted. God is wholly spiritual. Though Jewish folklore often pictures God as a king sitting on a heavenly throne, Jewish religious tradition does not take literally the image of God as king. The anthropomorphic terms which ascribe human characteristics to God were understood by the rabbis as a technique for explaining certain divine attributes to people unable to grasp abstractions.

It is difficult for human beings to grasp the reality of pure spirit. Many peoples have resorted to creating idols. They could see or touch an image or a statue; they could feel the reality of a god of wood or stone.

Judaism, however, has always defined itself in opposition to idolatry, whether it be the worship of graven images or the elevation of science, politics, or the ego above the worship of God.

Throughout the Bible, God, Moses, and the prophets exhort the Israelites to smash idols, to shun mere gods. They constantly warn the people about the dangers of succumbing to idolatry.

God is ethical: both just and loving, both righteous and compassionate. God is neither indifferent to human needs nor aloof from human affairs; rather, God insists that people live moral lives and fashion an ethical society. The rabbis explained the verse "You shall be holy for I, the Lord your God, am holy" (Leviticus 19:2) to mean "Just as He is merciful, you must be merciful; just as He is gracious, you must be gracious; just as He is truthful, you must be truthful; just as He is righteous, you must be righteous."

Morality is not simply an attribute that enables people to get along without destroying themselves. It is a divine imperative. The Creator designed a universe based on moral laws, and punishes those who break them. Jewish monotheism is an "ethical monotheism." It goes beyond faith in the existence of God, beyond the conviction that God is one. Its premise is that the One God is moral, demanding that His creatures act morally too.

## Teachings on the Afterlife

What happens if a people or a person refuses to act morally? Judaism teaches that God rewards and punishes human actions. Its teachings on the nature of reward and punishment, however, have changed greatly over the ages. In biblical days the emphasis was on group reward and group punishment (although the concept of individual reward and punishment also existed). A nation which disobeyed the divine commandments would suffer drought or famine or exile, but one which adhered to them would benefit from the bounties of nature and would prosper.

Later, when the doctrine of reward and punishment was applied to individuals, people began to notice that some wicked people seemed to prosper while some of the righteous suffered, and they wanted a more satisfactory explanation. The conviction that evil would be punished and good rewarded was transferred to the afterlife. If there seemed to be no reward and punishment in *this* world, they surely would be meted out in the next. Yet it is important to keep in mind that together with this concern about reward and punishment, Jewish tradition has always emphasized the obligation to live a worthy life for its own sake, free of insistence upon reward or fear of punishment. In the words of Rabbi Robert Gordis, "For the traditional believer, the full enjoyment of salvation is reserved for the world to come, but the achievement of salvation is a task to be accomplished in this world."

Nobody could spell out details about the afterlife. Those who spoke of Hell *(gehinnom)* never presented it as perpetual agonizing torment. Those who thought of a Devil *(Satan)* never conceived of him as an independent force capable of defying the Almighty; he was simply one of God's messengers. The different views regarding *gehinnom* are reflected in the divergent views of Shammai and Hillel, the two great masters of the first pre-Christian century. Shammai taught that upon death, the good dwell with God, the evil go to *gehinnom,* and those in between first go down and then come up to be healed after a time. Hillel disagreed, insisting that God's mercy would not permit Him to send any of His children to *gehinnom.*

Paradise was called the Garden of Eden *(gan eyden)*. It had no "pearly gates," no luxuriant gardens. It was not a place where sensual desires are gratified. The rabbis envisioned it as a place where people would be free of all physical needs and therefore able to spend their time in study. The third-century sage Rav taught: "The world to come is not like this world. There is no eating or drinking, no begetting of children, no bargaining, no jealousy, hatred or strife. The righteous sit with their crowns on their heads. What then will they eat and drink? The presence of God is food and drink to them."

The idea of immortality was always a Jewish concept, but all attempts to describe the specifics remained in the realm of legend. "To borrow an analogy from Maimonides," Rabbi Robert Gordis has written, "for us to conceive of life after death, an existence necessarily free from physical traits and attributes, is as impossible as for a color-blind person to grasp the colors of a sunset."

In modern times, many people have found it impossible to accept the idea of an actual heaven or hell. Nevertheless, they continue to believe in the doctrine of reward and punishment, in the teaching that goodness is somehow rewarded and that evil is somehow punished. Just as the rabbinic concept of reward and punishment retained that biblical idea but interpreted it differently, so some moderns think of it in nonphysical terms. They hold that one who acts wickedly creates his or her own hell on earth, while one who does right has an inner serenity and gratification that transcends all ill fortune.

This interpretation is strengthened by psychoanalytical and psychological insights which stress that every deed has its consequences, that even those which have no apparent impact leave an indelible imprint. It maintains that those who choose lives which reject religious morality may well suffer immeasurably, that those who choose ethical standards may well find inner rewards which are fulfilling. Judaism insists that there is a moral law operating in the universe and that whoever does not cooperate with that law pays the penalty.

## Teachings on Sin and Repentance

Judaism rejects the concept of Original Sin, the idea that human beings are inherently tainted. On the other hand, it is not so naive as to maintain that people are born inherently good, becoming corrupted solely because of external social forces. It recognizes both good and evil drives in the human makeup: *yetzer tov,* the good inclination, and *yetzer ra,* the evil inclination.

Which inclination will dominate a person, the *yetzer tov* or the *yetzer ra?* These inclinations exist in constant tension within each of us. God gave us the freedom to choose between them. Each person is responsible for his or her own conduct. The Book of Deuteronomy (30:19) declares: "Behold, I set before you this day life and good, death and evil. Therefore, choose life." God wants us to choose life, but leaves the decision to do so in our hands.

What happens when we do not make the proper choice, when, to use religious terminology, we sin? If our actions are the result of free will, each of us must be held personally accountable.

Judaism teaches that we can atone for our transgressions but that we cannot rely on intermediaries to make atonement for us. We cannot confess to a rabbi and receive absolution. Rabbis cannot perform that function because they are no closer to God than is any other Jew.

Instead, we must face God directly and atone for our own sins. We begin by recognizing our error. Then we admit it, confess it, and resolve never to repeat it. This process, called repentance *(teshuvah),* is the central theme and task of the High Holy Days *(Rosh Hashanah* and *Yom Kippur).*

## Teachings on the Concept of the Chosen People

The Bible is the sacred scripture of the Jewish people. It begins with the creation of Adam, of the human being. Adam is not white, black, red, or yellow. He is not Jew or Christian, not Muslim or Buddhist. He was created in the image of God. All people, all the descendants of Adam, contain the same divine spark; none are superior or inferior to any of the others. Any form of prejudice is a rejection of God. The commandment "You shall love your neighbor as yourself" (Leviticus 19:18) prohibits all prejudice.

While teaching that all people are God's children and that all nations are responsible before God, Judaism also teaches that the Jews have a special relationship with God. The Jewish people attained insights that others had not; they assumed responsibilities which others had not.

Indeed, tradition has it that God chose us as instruments through which His divine teachings are made known in the world. The Almighty gave the Torah to the world through the Jewish people, demanding that we live by its commandments in order to teach the world God's ways. God made a special covenant with us: He would be our God and we would be His people. To be part of this covenant, the Jews were to worship God alone, being faithful to God's laws. In turn, God would enable us to prosper in our own land. By serving our Ruler loyally, we would be "a light unto the nations."

Jews have always maintained that this special covenant which God made with us has defined us as a "chosen people." During religious services, the people honored by being called to stand by the Torah as it is read recite a special blessing *(berakhah)* which praises God "who has chosen us from among all peoples by giving us His Torah." The sacred days of the Jewish year are ushered in with a blessing which praises God "who has chosen us and distinguished us by adding holiness to our lives with His *mitzvot* (religious demands)."

"Chosenness" is both a distinction and a burden. It implies a special relationship and a special obligation. Once God revealed Himself to the Jewish people at Mt. Sinai, teaching them His laws and His ways, they were expected to reflect godliness constantly in their behavior. What may be excused for the uninitiated and uncommitted cannot be excused for those who have entered the covenant. This concept of chosenness has no connotation of religious or ethnic superiority. Being a member of the "Chosen People" gives no one a divine right to lord it over others. Rather, it entails a special responsibility to follow God's commandments.

Being a Jew implies concern for the physical and spiritual well-being of the Jewish people, but not for them alone. Judaism does not view universalism and particularism as being mutually exclusive. Jews must care about all human beings, just as they must care about the Jewish people. Traditionally, Jews have believed that you cannot promote your own welfare through narrow chauvinism, and that you cannot effectively advance the cause of society at large without a strong sense of your own identity.

## Teachings on Ethics

### THE SANCTITY OF LIFE

Judaism maintains that every human being is created in the divine image, that every life is inviolate and holy.

The Mishnah records:

> The Bible relates that God created Adam, a single human being, as the ancestor of all mankind. This teaches us that to destroy a single life is to destroy a whole world, even as to save a single life is to save a whole world. That all people have a common ancestor should make for peace, since no one can say to anyone else: "My father was greater than your father." That mankind began with a single human being is an answer to heretics who could claim the existence of more than one Creator. That mankind began with a single human being proclaims forever the greatness of the Holy One. For man stamps many coins with one die and they all look alike, but the Holy One stamped every human being with the die of Adam, yet no person is like any other. Therefore, every human being must declare, "It is for my sake that the world was created."

According to Jewish tradition, everything possible must be done to prolong and to improve life. Both individuals and the community have a responsibility to care for the sick, the aged, and the unproductive. They should never be abandoned.

Even animal life is precious. Jewish law forbids hunting for sport. Animals may be killed only for food (and then only according to specific laws designed to minimize fear and pain).

Although the commandments are of utmost importance, all

but three may be waived if death would be the consequence of obedience. The three which may never be transgressed are the prohibitions against the denial of God, sexual immorality, and murder.

The sixth commandment states, "You shall not *murder*"; it does not state, "Do not kill." Jewish tradition permits people to defend themselves when attacked. Judaism contains pacifist strains, but it teaches that some battles are not evil. At times it would be a greater evil not to fight than to fight. Submitting to Hitler, for example, would have been a far greater sin than fighting his forces. Allowing terrorists to kill people would be a greater wrong than fighting to prevent their attacks. When acquiescence means death, people are obliged to fight to save lives.

But in the absence of alternatives, the inevitable is performed with sadness. Golda Meir once said that when peace with the Arabs finally came, she would be able to forgive them everything except "forcing us to kill them."

The Jewish tradition has never gloried in military victories. At the Passover Seder, when Jews celebrate their delivery from ancient Egyptian slavery, we always pour out a few drops of wine from the cup to symbolize our sadness over the loss of Egyptian lives. King David, from whom, tradition tells us, the Messiah will be descended, was not permitted to build the Temple of the Lord in Jerusalem because he was a soldier with bloodstained hands. Judah the Maccabee led a small band of men in victorious attacks against superior forces and saved the Temple from the Hellenists, yet his military exploits do not dominate the religious ritual commemorating Hanukkah.

When the Israeli troops returned home after their brilliant triumph in the Six Day War of 1967, there were no victory parades, no cheering throngs. General Yitzhak Rabin eloquently described the people's reaction.

> The joy of our soldiers is incomplete and their celebrations are marred by sorrow and shock. There are some who abstain from

all celebration. The men in the front lines were witness not only
to the glory of victory, but the price of victory: their comrades
who fell beside them bleeding. The terrible price which our enemies paid touched the hearts of many of our men as well. It may
be that the Jewish people never learned and never accustomed itself to feel the triumph of conquest and victory, and we receive it
with mixed feeling.

The prophet Isaiah describes a Jewish vision of peace:

He will judge among the nations and arbitrate for many peoples,
And they shall beat their swords into plowshares
And their spears into pruning hooks.
Nation shall not take up sword against nation;
They shall never again know war. (Isaiah 2:4)

The rabbis further developed the idea. They declared that the
universe rests on three pillars: truth, justice, and peace. The last
passage of the *Amidah,* the central prayer of the three daily services, asks God for the blessing of peace *(shalom).* The Mishnah
closes with the statement that God has chosen peace as the best
instrument with which to bless the people Israel.

JUSTICE
Peace alone, precious as it is, cannot maintain a good society. The
Hebrew word for peace, *shalom,* connotes more than the absence
of warfare. It means fullness, completeness, the presence of well-
being. Peace cannot exist in a society that is not just. The passion for justice permeates Jewish tradition. The Bible com-
mands: "Justice, justice shall you pursue," making social justice a
religious requirement. The Jewish legal system protects the
rights of the individual; the ethical system teaches that a society
which permits exploitation, poverty, and ignorance defies God's
teachings and will suffer His wrath.

## TZEDAKAH

The passion for justice is expressed in the concept of *tzedakah*. The word means much more than charity; it means justice. Charity is something given by someone to another who has less. *Tzedakah* is more than a gift; it is an act of justice. Helping others is fulfilling one's duty, not simply an act of kindness. Everything on earth belongs to God. We are obliged to share with others whatever portion of it we happen to control.

In Jewish tradition, being poor is not considered an expression of piety; nor is being wealthy a sign of virtue. Jews regard poverty as a cause of suffering which should be eradicated. Jewish teachings about social justice implant a sense of responsibility in everyone.

A portion of the Mishnah which is read daily during morning prayer states:

> These are the deeds which yield immediate fruit and continue to yield fruit in time to come: honoring parents, doing deeds of lovingkindness, attending the house of study punctually, morning and evening, providing hospitality, visiting the sick, helping the needy bride, providing a funeral for the dead, probing the meaning of prayer, and making peace between one person and another.

In Talmudic times, everyone had to contribute to a common fund which was used to maintain a free soup kitchen, to provide lodging for travelers, and to help the unfortunate. Special organizations provided poor brides with dowries, tended the sick, lent money without interest, and took care of the dead. Employers were expected to pay their workers on time and were not to take advantage of them.

That emphasis on social justice was translated into communal institutions which functioned in all Jewish communities. Taking care of the needy is a sacred obligation. Even in Western democracies, where participation in Jewish life is voluntary rather than obligatory, *tzedakah* has remained the prime concern of all identified Jews. Jewish Federations in every community raise tremendous sums for local and national needs as well as for Israel and for other Jews throughout the world. Individuals not pleased with the way the Federations allocate funds arrange alternative contributions. Jews who may not look upon themselves as "religious" and who may know nothing of Jewish law or lore nevertheless faithfully carry out the responsibility of *tzedakah*.

## MERCY

According to Jewish understanding, a society cannot exist without justice, but justice alone can be dispatched heartlessly unless it is tempered with mercy. God, extolled as just, is praised as merciful. Following God's ways, we are obliged to be loving as well as righteous. We should not only refrain from condoning wrongs; we should strive to be compassionate and sympathetic.

## THE OPTIMISM OF JUDAISM

Judaism has been described as an optimistic religion. It teaches that we are capable of being just and merciful, of improving ourselves and our society. One of the best-known prayers, *Aleinu,* which is recited at the end of every service, expresses the yearning to perfect this world through God's kingship.

There have, of course, been periods in Jewish history when Jews passively awaited divine intervention, through the Messiah, to bring them a just society. Usually, however, they have felt impelled to take action themselves. They have never been frozen into despair that their dream might never be realized.

Nor did they relegate their vision of perfection to the afterlife. Although most Jews in premodern times believed in the existence of another world, their Judaism was essentially focused on *this* world. It did not minimize social problems by looking to the world to come. It did not seek escape from this world, as some Eastern religions did. Even Jewish mystics who could find religious ecstasy only in solitude married, raised families, prayed in a synagogue with others, and took some active role in the life of the community.

Judaism insists that every person assume the obligations of being a responsible member of society. By adhering to God's laws, and by correcting social wrongs rather than acquiescing to them, Jews can make the future better than the present.

This optimism may seem utopian, but Jewish tradition has constantly devised ways of giving concrete expression to abstract ideals. It has embodied them in a way of life guided by law *(ha-lakhah)*. The myriad details which are part of the code of law reflect the wisdom of the sages who understood that words mean little if they are not translated into deeds. If people profess love and practice cruelty, their profession is meaningless; if they preach charity and act miserly, their sincerity is questionable. As the rabbis declared, "It is not the preaching that counts, but the deed."

Although they could not legislate emotions or sincerity, the rabbis did work out rules of conduct which concretize principles and translate ideals into a way of life. They relied on a deep faith that God's spirit is at work in the world, inspiring men and women to become their best possible selves.

Not everyone succeeds; Judaism has always recognized that human beings are not perfect. We must never stop striving to attain the ideal. As the rabbis taught, "You are not obliged to complete the task, but you are not free to desist from it."

## Suggested Readings for Further Study

Gordis, Robert, *A Faith for Moderns* (New York: Bloch Publishing Company, 1960)

Kaplan, Mordecai, *Questions Jews Ask* (New York: Reconstructionist Press, 1956)

ADDITIONAL SUGGESTIONS

Jacobs, Louis, *Faith* (New York: Basic Books, 1968)

_____, *Jewish Values* (London: Valentine, Mitchell, 1960)

_____, *Principles of Jewish Faith* (New York: Basic Books, 1964)

_____, *We Have Reason to Believe* (London: Valentine, Mitchell, 1965)

Schwartz, Charles and Betty, *Faith through Reason* (New York, London and Toronto: Thomas Yoseloff, 1946)

Siegel, Seymour, and Gertel, Elliot, *God in the Teachings of Conservative Judaism* (New York: The Rabbinical Assembly, 1985)

CHAPTER 3

# Religious Movements in Judaism

THE Jewish faith is rooted in an ancient heritage, a millenia-old civilization. Nevertheless, it is not monolithic. There are different interpretations of the historic faith and the implications of its theology. Still, however they differed, all Jews remained part of the same covenant, members of the same people. Throughout history, there have been individuals and schools who disagreed with the teachings of opponents. They did so, however, without reading out of the fold those with whom they disagreed.

On the contemporary scene, there are four movements that have evolved to express different approaches to the tradition. They arose out of the need to respond to the challenges of modern times. After the French Revolution, Jews began to be admitted into the dominant society. Ghetto walls began to fall and Jews were permitted to share in the general culture.

This presented a dilemma. How could they be at home in the non-Jewish world without surrendering their own Jewish life, without transgressing their own laws and customs, without forfeiting their own language and educational system? Obviously, adjustments were necessary. The Jews had to find ways to take advantage of the new opportunities without surrendering their Jewish identities. They had to decide what had to be retained from the past and what could be deleted or modified. They did not all respond in the same way. The responses were structured into four separate movements.

## Reform Judaism

Most of the Jews of France and Germany joyfully welcomed the change in their status and the opportunity to be like other Germans and Frenchmen. They eagerly embraced the way of life of their fellow countrymen and sought to prove that they were worthy of emancipation. The most enthusiastic among them were prepared to abandon Judaism altogether, and some actually went through the formalities of converting to Christianity. Not theological conviction but the desire not to be different moved them to such a step. The great German-Jewish poet Heinrich Heine observed that baptism was "a ticket of admission into European society."

Most Jews refused to go so far. They were convinced that much of the past no longer needed to be perpetuated but they did not want everything abandoned. They introduced what were then regarded as radical innovations and thereby created Reform Judaism. They began using the organ at services, which was shocking to a people who had not used instrumental music at times of prayer since the days of the Temple in Jerusalem. They recited some prayers in German, insisted on Western standards of decorum, and introduced weekly sermons.

In the 1840s and 1850s, as the number of Reformers grew, their rabbis set about reshaping the very nature of Judaism. They declared it to be nothing more than a religious faith, and no longer saw it as the religious civilization of the Jewish people. They rejected all the group or national aspects of Judaism and proclaimed the Jews a religious communion rather than a people in exile. They eliminated everything that was not purely "spiritual," all the nationalistic practices and ideals. They dropped liturgical references to Jerusalem and prayers for the restoration of Zion. In the prayerbook, they substituted the vernacular for Hebrew. They saw Jewish law as history with no contemporary relevance and declared it no longer binding. Prophetic morality was the only element of the past which they thought was still valid. Indeed, they insisted, Jews were to remain Jews because they had a mission: to teach the moral principles of the Prophets to mankind. They saw everything else as particularistic, tribal customs which were no longer relevant. Some rabbis even shifted the Sabbath from Saturday to Sunday, and advised eliminating circumcision as a sign of the covenant. The majority, however, refused to go to such extremes. Reform synagogues (or "temples") became imitations of liberal churches; Reform homes lost all traces of traditional Jewishness.

When Reform came to America, it grew and became even more radical than it had been in Germany, the country of its origins. It became a movement when its rabbis organized themselves and their congregations and established a school. They conducted dignified and decorous services. They eliminated whatever struck them as archaic. They were indifferent and sometimes antagonistic to folk celebrations and ritual observances. They emphasized the prophetic demand for social justice and morality. The movement possessed a great strength: it allowed for self-criticism and change when deemed desirable. When several Reform thinkers concluded that the break with the past had gone too far, they set about bringing Reform Judaism closer to the tradition.

By the mid-1930s most Reform Jews accepted the principle of Jewish peoplehood. Whereas most of the early Reformers had been bitter anti-Zionists, the majority increasingly accepted the need for a Jewish state. Since the birth of the State of Israel, only a very small minority has remained hostile, and an ever-increasing majority has become wholly committed to its survival. Re-

form Jews are now introducing more Hebrew into services as well
as into schools.

A few voices have recently been raised urging some kind of
code of religious behavior, though Reform as a whole continues
to believe that Jewish law is not binding. Reform Jews are not
required to observe the dietary laws *(kashrut),* although some of
them choose not to eat pork, which is explicitly prohibited in the
Bible. The attitude toward ritual observances, however, is no
longer negative, and those who wish to adopt some of them feel
comfortable doing so.

Reform authorities have edited and revised the liturgy ex-
tensively. Most of the prayers are recited in English at a service
which often includes organ music and a choir. In most Reform
congregations, men do not wear the traditional *yarmulke* or prayer
shawl, nor do they put on *tefillin.* Recent editions of the Reform
prayerbook, published by the Central Conference of American
Rabbis, have included traditional texts.

## *Orthodox Judaism*

Other Jews who were attracted by the European culture opening
up before them had a different point of view. They also wanted
to participate in cultural life (to attend the universities, to go to
the theater, read secular literature), but not at the price of relin-
quishing the observance of Jewish law. They adhered to their
traditional belief that the Torah had been revealed to Moses by
God on Mount Sinai and that all of its instructions are eternally
binding. They also believed that all of the subsequent religious
law developed by the rabbis is an expression of divine will, not
subject to change by any modern interpretation which is not authoritative for them. The foremost proponent of this school of
thought, neo-Orthodoxy, was Rabbi Samson Raphael Hirsch.
His book *The Nineteen Letters of Ben Uzziel* is the best popular
presentation of this philosophy.

Neo-Orthodoxy was not universally accepted, however. The

Orthodoxy of Eastern Europe differed, sharing the deep commitment to Jewish law, but without interest in active involvement in any part of secular culture. These Eastern European Jews refused to countenance any adaptation and regarded the sixteenth-century code of law the *Shulḥan Arukh* as their guiding legal authority. They have maintained all the details of their religious regimen as well as a traditional outlook on life. Some of the most extreme wear the kind of garb worn by their ancestors for centuries. They frown on secular education and teach only those subjects required by the government. The so-called modern Orthodox, on the other hand, are integrated into Western culture while faithfully adhering to all of Jewish law.

Services in Orthodox congregations are in Hebrew, with English responsive readings used occasionally in some of them. The sermon is usually given in the vernacular. The liturgy is the same as it has been for centuries. There may be slight variations from congregation to congregation, but these stem from local practices developed in different parts of Europe, not from ideological differences. Men and married women keep their heads covered at all times. Women sit in separate sections of the synagogue. They do not participate in the conduct of the service in any way other than following the service from their seats.

The Orthodox are punctilious about observing all aspects of Jewish law, adhering strictly to rabbinic law as it is interpreted by Orthodox authorities.

## Conservative Judaism

A third interpretation of the Jewish religion also emerged in Germany and developed in the United States. The adherents of Conservative Judaism agreed with some of the theses of both Reform and Orthodox Judaism and disagreed with others. On the one hand, the Conservative movement insists that Jewish law is binding. On the other hand, the Conservative movement finds within Jewish history a process of evolution, the absorption of the changes and adaptations made in every era in response to new realities, new ideas, and new perceptions of the world. Changes in the interpretation of Jewish law, rooted in and consistent with Jewish practice, have been made according to the tradition of development built into Jewish law. Conservative Judaism has been characterized by both its insistence on tradition and its openness to change.

The process of interpreting Jewish law is ongoing. Conservative Jews, in contradistinction to Orthodox Jews, may, for example, use electricity on Shabbat through a ruling which distinguishes electricity from fire (which may not be kindled on Shabbat). Conservative Jews are permitted to ride on Shabbat, but solely for the purpose of attending synagogue services and returning home. The dietary laws are regarded as sacred, but the Committee on Jewish Law and Standards of the Rabbinical Assembly (the Conservative movement's rabbinical organization) has ruled that nonmeat products (except for nonkosher fish, such as shellfish) may be eaten at facilities which serve nonkosher food.

Conservative Jews also believe deeply that Judaism is the particular religion of a particular people. They therefore stress the study of Hebrew, the traditional language of the Jewish people, and emphasize the importance of the land of Israel as the national home of the people and its religion. The liturgy thus is largely in Hebrew, with varying proportions of English depending upon local practice. The basic pattern of the liturgy is traditional, and the references to Zion are retained, but some ideological changes have been made and new compositions added. In many congregations, women take an active part in the services.

## Reconstructionist Judaism

A fourth movement in Judaism emerged in the United States in 1934. Reconstructionism is the fruit of the thinking of Rabbi Mordecai M. Kaplan who, though long identified with the Conservative movement and professor at its Jewish Theological Seminary for more than half a century, found the other three approaches wanting. In his vision of the totality of Judaism, he defined Judaism as "the evolving religious civilization" of the Jewish people. "Evolving" means that Judaism is not static, that it has always developed and grown. "Religious" means that the main emphasis of Jewish civilization has been religious, that it has been concerned primarily with God and spiritual living. "Civilization" means that Judaism is more than a religion, that it is a total way of life encompassing folkways and mores, a common history and common aspirations, a language and a relationship to a special land, a religion and a legal system.

Rabbi Kaplan rejected supernaturalism; his position was that of "religious humanism." He conceived of God as a Power, not as a person. He even dared to define God as "the Power that makes for salvation" and "the Power that drives man on to make the most of himself." He accordingly removed from the prayerbook all supernaturalist expressions as well as those deemed *passé*. Nevertheless, Reconstructionist liturgy follows the traditional pattern and reflects the traditional intertwining of peoplehood and religion although it does introduce basic changes and reinterpretations into the text of the prayerbook. Reconstructionists no longer accept Jewish law *(halakhah)* as binding, but they observe traditional practices which they consider to be expressions of the Jewish religious civilization.

For many years, the Reconstructionists were considered the left wing of the Conservative movement, and those who accepted Rabbi Kaplan's philosophy belonged to either the Conservative or the Reform movements. Most continue to do so even though there are now Reconstructionist congregations, the Reconstructionist Rabbinical Association, and the Reconstructionist Rabbinical College. Many American Jewish leaders are unable to accept Rabbi Kaplan's theology, but all have been affected deeply by his analysis of contemporary Jewish life and his prescriptions for curing its ills.

## Movements, Not Denominations

The Reform, Orthodox, Conservative, and Reconstructionist movements are not parallel to the various groupings within Protestantism; they are not separate denominations. There are differences among them, but all Jews, including secularists, are members of the Jewish people.

The liturgical and ritual differences among these groups center principally on the interpretation of Jewish law. The varied practices stem from the fact that both Reform and Reconstructionism maintain that Jewish law *(halakhah)* is no longer binding, while Orthodox and Conservative Jews insist that it is.

## Suggested Readings for Further Study

Kaufman, William, *Contemporary Jewish Philosophers* (New York: Reconstructionist Press and Behrman House, 1976)

Raphael, Marc Lee, *Profiles in American Judaism* (San Francisco: Harper and Row, 1984)

Rosenthal, Gilbert, *Four Paths to One God* (New York: Bloch Publishing Company, 1973)

_____, *Patterns of Survival* (New York: Human Sciences Press, 1985)

ADDITIONAL SUGGESTIONS

Borowitz, Eugene, *Reform Judaism Today* (New York: Behrman House, 1978)

Dorff, Elliot N., *Conservative Judaism: Our Ancestors to Our Descendants* (New York: The United Synagogue, 1977)

Eisenstein, Ira, *Varieties of Religious Belief* (New York: Reconstructionist Press, 1966)

Gordis, Robert, *Understanding Conservative Judaism* (New York: The Rabbinical Assembly, 1978)

Kaplan, Mordecai, M., *Questions Jews Ask* (New York: Reconstructionist Press, 1956)

Lamm, Norman, and Wurzburger, Walter S., editors, *A Treasury of Tradition* (New York: Hebrew Publishing Co., 1967)

Rackman, Emanuel, *One Man's Judaism* (New York: Philosophical Library, 1970)

Schwartzman, Sylvan, *Reform Judaism Then and Now* (New York: Union of American Hebrew Congregations, 1971)

Waxman, Mordecai, editor, *Tradition and Change* (New York: The Burning Bush Press, 1958)

# CHAPTER 4

# How Do Jews Worship?

*H*ow do you get to feel at home in the world of Jewish prayer? It might seem simple at first—just go to a synagogue, pick up the prayerbook, and follow the service! That, however, is easier said than done. Not that it is difficult to find a prayerbook. Every synagogue has copies available. But following the services and understanding the prayers are another matter. Many words and phrases, chants and melodies will seem strange at first. Few, if any, translations are able to convey the true meaning and emotional impact of the words absorbed and felt by the people who are reciting them in Hebrew.

The best way of learning to feel comfortable with Jewish worship begins with getting to know the prayerbook, the *Siddur*. To understand it, you will need to study it, not just glance through it.

Understanding the *Siddur* will bring you to the heart of Judaism. If you want to know what Jews should believe, there is no better text than the prayerbook. It is *the* book of Jewish theology. The *Siddur* contains the three services—morning, afternoon, and evening—for weekdays and for Shabbat and Festivals (with an additional service added for each of the last two occasions). It also contains prayers and blessings which observant Jews recite at significant times in their personal lives and throughout the weeks and years of the liturgical year and contains as well blessings occasioned by daily occurences. More than any other single volume, the *Siddur* contains the beliefs and teachings of the Jewish people, expressing the yearnings of the Jew and the Jewish tradition. It conveys the historic hopes, the religious longings, and the spiritual ideals of the Jewish people.

The *Siddur* is not the product of any one person or of any one age. It records the religious creativity of an entire people throughout the ages. It contains passages from the Bible and the Talmud, from medieval poets, and, in some editions, from modern and contemporary thinkers. All Jews have followed the same basic core of the service, but different communities have supplemented this core with liturgical poems and other selections, often modifying and adding to the text.

The prayerbook you will find in a synagogue will reflect the ideology of the movement with which that synagogue identifies. Reform, Orthodox, Conservative, and Reconstructionist individuals or movements have published prayerbooks reflecting their interpretations of the Jewish tradition. You will find several of them listed in the bibliography at the end of this chapter.

According to Jewish law, people may pray in any language they understand. Most prayerbooks printed in the West have translations on the pages facing the Hebrew. Jews, for the most part, have found that only Hebrew authentically expresses the Jewish soul, with its own nuances and emotional impact. Moreover, the use of Hebrew binds Jews to past generations and to Jews in other lands. The use of Hebrew persists in services, even though many people do not know the meaning of most words. Virtually every *Siddur* contains all or part of the service in Hebrew.

## *The Evening Service—Maariv, or Arvit*

We begin by studying the evening service because it is the first service of the Jewish day, which begins at sundown. It is called *maariv,* or *arvit* (the Hebrew word for evening is *erev*).

Each part of the service is known by its Hebrew name. The service begins with the leader chanting a formal call to prayer *(Barkhu),* translated as: "Praise the Lord, Source of blessing." The congregation responds: "Praised be the Lord, Source of blessing throughout all time." The service continues with two longer passages which are *berakhot,* blessings, expressing basic Jewish convictions about the universe. The first *berakhah* praises God for His gift of Creation.

> Praised are You, Lord our God, King of the universe whose word brings on the evening dusk. You open the gates of dawn with wisdom, change the day's divisions with understanding, set the succession of seasons and arrange the stars in the sky according to Your will. You create day and night, rolling light away from darkness and darkness away from light. Eternal God, Your rule shall embrace us forever. Praised are You, Lord, for each evening's dusk.

The next *berakhah* praises God for His gift of Revelation, Torah, sign of His love.

> With constancy You have loved Your people Israel, teaching us Torah and mitzvot, statutes and laws. Therefore, Lord our God, when we lie down to sleep and when we rise, we shall think of Your laws and speak of them, rejoicing in Your Torah and mitzvot always. For they are our life and length of days; we will meditate upon them day and night. Never take away Your love from us. Praised are You, Lord who loves His people Israel.

The service next proclaims the Oneness of God in the central prayer of Jewish faith: the *Sh'ma*. The name *Sh'ma* is taken from the first Hebrew word of a verse from Deuteronomy (6:4): *Sh'ma yisrael Adonai Eloheinu Adonai eḥad,* "Hear, O Israel: The Lord our God, the Lord is One." This declaration of faith is the first prayer that children learn; and it is the passage prescribed by tradition to be among the last words uttered before death.

It is more than a simple declaration of belief in God, who is one. It is also a way of looking at the universe. If God is one, then all human beings are God's children, united in one family. If God is one, history is not a series of isolated episodes but of events related to each other with meaning and purpose. Moreover, if God is one, the forces of nature are part of a whole, not random. By proclaiming "God is one," the Jew is asserting faith in the unity of all people, the importance of human history, and the harmony of a natural world which is hospitable to human beings.

After the verse from Deuteronomy cited above, the service continues with a passage from an ancient rabbinic tradition which proclaims ultimate allegiance to God alone and accepts the obligation to serve Him: "Praised be His glorious sovereignty throughout all time."

This section, known as *K'riat Sh'ma,* continues with Deuteronomy 6:5–9.

> Love the Lord your God with all your heart, with all your soul, with all your might. And these words which I command you this day you shall take to heart. You shall diligently teach them to your children. You shall recite them at home and away, morning and night. You shall bind them as a sign upon your hand, they shall be a symbol above your eyes, and you shall inscribe them upon the doorposts of your homes and upon your gates.

To fulfill this last commandment we place a *mezuzah,* a small case containing a parchment scroll, on our doorposts. It contains the words of the first two passages of *K'riat Sh'ma.* Each time we pass through a door which has a *mezuzah,* we are reminded of the values expressed on the scroll within it.

The second passage of *K'riat Sh'ma* (Deuteronomy 11:13–21) is concerned with the theological premise that good is rewarded and evil punished, presenting the earliest formulation of this doctrine.

The third passage is Numbers 15:37–41.

> The Lord said to Moses: Instruct the people Israel that in every generation they shall put fringes on the corners of their garments and bind a thread of blue to the fringe of each corner. Looking upon it, you will be reminded of all the mitzvot of the Lord and fulfill them and not be seduced by your heart or led astray by your eyes. Then you will remember and observe all My mitzvot and be holy before your God. I am the Lord your God who brought you out of the land of Egypt to be your God. I, the Lord, am your God.

When styles changed and four-cornered garments were no longer worn, Jews substituted a prayer shawl *(tallit)* with four corners to which *tzitzit* are attached. The purposes of *tzitzit* remains the same: to remind people to live by divine law.

Just as *K'riat Sh'ma* of the evening service is introduced by two *berakhot,* it is followed by two. The first praises God for redeeming us from Egyptian bondage. The Exodus from Egypt is often recalled in the liturgy, because that momentous event has been taken as evidence that God was, is, and will be the Redeemer of the people Israel. The second *berakhah* praises God for His peace and protection.

After *K'riat Sh'ma,* and its accompanying *berakhot,* the evening service continues with a prayer so basic that it is referred to as "*the* prayer." It is recited at every service, and it is known by two Hebrew names. One is *Amidah,* a Hebrew word that means "standing," for it is recited while standing *(K'riat Sh'ma,* on the other hand, is recited while seated). The other is *Shmoneh Esreh,* a Hebrew word meaning "eighteen," since the original *Amidah* consisted of eighteen *berakhot.* (It now comprises nineteen *berakhot* because the rabbis added an additional *berakhah* in Tal-

mudic times.) The first three and the last three *berakhot* of the
*Amidah* are the same for weekday, Sabbath, and Festival services.

The first *berakhah* is called *Avot* (ancestors) because it mentions the God of Abraham, Isaac, and Jacob—that is, the God of
history.

> Praised are You, Lord our God and God of our ancestors, God
> of Abraham, of Isaac and of Jacob, great, mighty, awesome, ex-
> alted God, bestowing lovingkindness, Creator of all. You remem-
> ber the pious deeds of our ancestors and will send a redeemer to
> their children's children because of Your loving nature. You are
> the King who helps and saves and shields. Praised are You, Lord,
> Shield of Abraham.

Though each generation may conceive of God in a different
way, God remains the same throughout all time. One rabbi made
this point by indicating that the text reads "God of Abraham, of
Isaac, and of Jacob," rather than "God of Abraham, Isaac, and
Jacob." God is related directly to each, since each emphasized a
different aspect of the same God. Each brought God into his life
in his own way. Just as each of the Patriarchs may have recognized a different aspect of God, so may we.

The second *berakhah* is known as *Gevurot,* referring to God's
mighty deeds.

> Your might, O Lord, is boundless. You give life to the dead;
> great is Your saving power. Your lovingkindness sustains the liv-
> ing. Your great mercies give life to the dead. You support the
> falling, heal the ailing, free the fettered. You keep Your faith with
> those who sleep in dust. Whose power can compare with Yours?
> You are the Master of life and death and deliverance. Faithful are
> You in giving life to the dead. Praised are You, Lord, Master of
> life and death.

The belief in physical resurrection has been held by many
Jews throughout the centuries, but not all Jews have accepted it

literally. Without changing the time-honored words of the Hebrew *berakhah,* some modern authorities have reinterpreted the
concept to mean a nonphysical immortality. Others, unwilling to
read such meaning into the traditional phrases, have changed the
wording.

The third *berakhah* of the *Amidah* is called *Kedushah,* "holiness."

> Holy are You and holy is Your name. Holy are those who praise
> You daily. Praised are You, Lord, holy God.

We will skip the intermediate section of *berakhot* now, to
present the three concluding *berakhot* of the *Amidah.* The first of
these is called *Avodah* (worship):

> Accept the prayer of Your people as lovingly as it is offered. Re-
> store worship to Your sanctuary. May the worship of Your peo-
> ple Israel always be acceptable to You. May we witness Your
> merciful return to Zion. Praised are You, Lord who restores His
> Presence to Zion.

Ever since the Romans destroyed the Temple in the year 70 C.E.,
Jews have yearned to return to Zion and to rebuild the Sanctuary. This prayer kept alive in the hearts of Jewry the passionate
longing for a reborn Jewish Commonwealth in which they would
be free to worship God in their own manner. Though compar-
atively few people today want to restore the Temple cult (with
its ritual of animal sacrifice), they recite the *Avodah* because it expresses their deep love for Zion.

The next passage is referred to as *Hodayah* (grateful ac-
knowledgement):

> We proclaim that You are the Lord our God and God of our
> ancestors throughout all time. You are the Rock of our lives, the
> Shield of our salvation in every generation. We thank You and
> praise You morning, noon, and night for Your miracles which

daily attend us and for Your wondrous kindnesses. Our lives are
in Your hand; our souls are in Your charge. You are good, with
everlasting mercy; You are compassionate, with enduring lovingkindness. We have always placed our hope in You. For all these
blessings we shall praise and exalt You. May every living creature
thank You and praise You faithfully, our deliverance and our
help. Praised are You, beneficent Lord to whom all praise is due.

The last *berakhah* is called *Shalom* because it is a prayer for
true peace, which Judaism has always regarded as the greatest
blessing.

Grant peace to the world, with happiness, and blessing, grace,
love and mercy for us and for all the people Israel. Bless us, our
Father, one and all, with Your light; for by that light did You
teach us Torah and life, love and tenderness, justice, mercy, and
peace. May it please You to bless Your people Israel in every season and at all times with Your gift of peace. Praised are You,
Lord who blesses His people Israel with peace.

We now introduce the intermediate passages. On weekdays
they consist of thirteen petitions, beginning with a request for
knowledge.

You graciously endow mortals with intelligence, teaching wisdom
and understanding. Grant us knowledge, discernment, and wisdom. Praised are You, Lord who graciously grants intelligence.

This is followed by *berakhot* with the themes of repentance, forgiveness, redemption, healing, good crops, ingathering of the
dispersed, justice, humbling the arrogant, and sustaining the
righteous:

Our Father, bring us back to Your Torah. Our King, draw us
near to Your service. Lead us back to You, truly repentant.
Praised are You, Lord who welcomes repentance.

Forgive us, our Father, for we have sinned; pardon us, our King, for we have transgressed, for You forgive and pardon. Praised are You, gracious and forgiving Lord.

Behold our afflictions and deliver us. Redeem us soon because of Your mercy, for You are the mighty Redeemer. Praised are You, Lord, Redeemer of the people Israel.

Heal us, O Lord, and we shall be healed. Help us and save us, for You are our glory. Grant perfect healing for all our afflictions. For You are the faithful and merciful God of healing. Praised are You, Lord, Healer of His people Israel.

Lord our God, make this a blessed year. May its varied produce bring us happiness. Grant blessing to the earth. Satisfy us with its abundance, and bless our year as the best of years. Praised are You, Lord who blesses the years.

Sound the great shofar to herald our freedom, raise high the banner to gather our exiles. Gather our dispersed from the ends of the earth. Praised are You, Lord who gathers our dispersed.

Restore our judges as in days of old, restore our counselors as in former times. Remove from us sorrow and anguish. Reign alone over us with lovingkindness; with justice and mercy sustain our cause. Praised are You, King who loves justice.

Frustrate the hopes of all those who malign us; let all evil very soon disappear. Let all Your enemies soon be destroyed. May You quickly uproot and crush the arrogant; may You subdue and humble them in our time. Praised are You, Lord who humbles the arrogant.

Let Your tender mercies be stirred for the righteous, the pious, and the leaders of the House of Israel, devoted scholars and faithful proselytes. Be merciful to us of the House of Israel. Reward all who trust in You, cast our lot with those who are faithful to You. May we never come to despair, for our trust is in You. Praised are You, Lord who sustains the righteous.

The *Amidah* continues with petitions for the rebuilding of

Jersusalem, the advent of the Messianic Era, and for the answering of prayer:

> Have mercy, Lord, and return to Jerusalem, Your city. May Your Presence dwell there as You have promised. Build it now, in our days and for all time. Reestablish there the majesty of David, Your servant. Praised are You, Lord who builds Jerusalem.
>
> Bring to flower the shoot of Your servant David. Hasten the advent of Messianic redemption. Each and every day we hope for Your deliverance. Praised are You, Lord who assures our deliverance.
>
> Lord our God, hear our voice. Have compassion upon us, pity us, accept our prayer with loving favor. You listen to entreaty and prayer. Do not turn us away unanswered, our King, for You mercifully heed Your people's supplication. Praised are You, Lord who hears prayer.

These thirteen intermediate passages are not recited on the Sabbath or on Festivals, for the concerns over such requests are not felt to be appropriate on days devoted to joy and celebration. The intermediate section of the *Amidah* on those days, consisting of a single *berakhah,* articulates the theme of the Sabbath or Festival, extolling the special sanctity of the day being observed.

Every service concludes with a passage known as *Aleinu,* which is its first Hebrew word:

> We rise to our duty to praise the Lord of all, to acclaim the Creator. He made our lot unlike that of other people, assigning to us a unique destiny. We bend the knee and bow, acknowledging the King of kings, the Holy One praised be He, who spread out the heavens and laid the foundations of the earth, whose glorious abode is in the highest heaven, whose mighty dominion is in the loftiest heights. He is our God, there is no other. In truth, He alone is our King, as it is written in His Torah: "Know this day

and take it to heart that the Lord is God in heaven above and on earth below; there is no other."

And so we hope in You, Lord our God, soon to see Your splendor, sweeping idolatry away so that false gods will be utterly destroyed, perfecting the earth by Your kingship so that all mankind will invoke Your name, bringing all the earth's wicked back to You, repentant. Then all who live will know that to You every knee must bend, every tongue pledge loyalty. To You, Lord, may all bow in worship, may they give honor to Your glory. May everyone accept the rule of Your kingship. Reign over all, soon and for all time. Sovereignty is Yours in glory, now and forever. Thus is it written in Your Torah: "The Lord reigns forever and ever." Such is the assurance of Your prophet Zechariah: "The Lord shall be acknowledged King of the earth. On that day the Lord shall be One and His name One."

The first passage of *Aleinu* accepts the duty to praise the Lord of all, who fashioned the Jews as a distinct people. The second part proclaims the universality of God and looks forward to the time when all humanity will accept ultimate allegiance to God alone. *Aleinu* declares that we must actively participate in trying to perfect society.

The Mourner's *Kaddish* is recited after *Aleinu*. It is not mournful in content. By reciting it the mourner affirms praise of our Creator, an act of affirming faith in God at moments of greatest trial and doubt.

Hallowed and enhanced may He be throughout the world of His own creation. May He cause His sovereignty soon to be accepted, during our life and the life of all Israel. And let us say: Amen.

*Congregational response:* May He be praised throughout all time.

Glorified and celebrated, lauded and worshiped, acclaimed and honored, extolled and exalted may the Holy One be, praised beyond all song and psalm, beyond all tributes which mortals can utter. And let us say: Amen.

Let there be abundant peace from Heaven, with life's goodness for us and for all the people Israel. And let us say: Amen.

He who brings peace to His universe will bring peace to us and to all the people Israel. And let us say: Amen.

In most Reform congregations, everyone rises to recite the Mourner's *Kaddish*. In other congregations, the Mourner's *Kaddish* is a personal affirmation made by those individuals who have suffered a loss, so only mourners and those observing the anniversary of a death *(yahrzeit)* rise to recite it.

The prayer leader recites the *Kaddish* in slightly different forms to separate certain sections of the service. The Christian prayer known as "The Lord's Prayer" is rooted in the *Kaddish,* with many identical and similar phrases.

The Mourner's *Kaddish* concludes the formal, prescribed service. Most congregations, however, add a liturgical poem which is sung as a conclusion. By and large, this practice is followed on Sabbaths and Festivals, not on weekdays. One commonly used poem is *Adon Olam,* a hymn of praise to the eternal Lord, our Creator in whom we place our trust. Another is *Yigdal,* a poetic paraphrase of the Thirteen Principles of Faith formulated by Maimonides.

### *The Morning Service—Shaḥarit*

The core of this service is similar to that of *Maariv.* It is a longer service, however, beginning with Morning *Berakhot (Birkhot Hashaḥar),* a section celebrating the renewal of life on a new day. This section expresses gratitude and praise for God's gifts of body and soul, as well as for His compassion, for our covenant with Him, and for the Torah. Passages from the Torah and from rabbinic literature are included to fulfill the minimal obligation for daily study. The next section, known as *Pesukei Dezimra* (Passages of Praise), contains psalms and passages from other books of the Bible. It is the intention of the liturgy that the recitation of these two sections will help the worshiper "to approach the core of the morning prayer service in the proper spirit, with an informed heart, freely, openly and gladly."

The rest of the service is similar to *Maariv,* including a formal call to worship *(Barkhu), K'riat Sh'ma* and its *berakhot* and the *Amidah.* As at *Maariv, K'riat Sh'ma* is preceded by two *berakhot* which express gratitude to God for Creation and for Revelation, but it is followed by only one *berakhah,* with the theme of Redemption.

The *Amidah* is followed by a short reading from the Torah on Mondays and Thursdays (these were the market days in ancient Israel, appropriate times for teaching the Torah in public). *Aleinu* and the Mourner's *Kaddish* conclude the service.

## The Afternoon Service—Minḥah

This is the briefest service of the day. The word *minḥah* means "gift." This service recalls the afternoon sacrifice *(minḥah)* offered in the ancient Temple. The *Minḥah* Service generally is held just before the Evening Service. Some synagogues have introduced a study session to separate these two services.

*K'riat Sh'ma* and its *berakhot* are not recited, but the *Amidah* is, preceded by Psalm 145 (known by the Hebrew word, *Ashrei,* the first word of a passage added from another psalm). Psalm 145 sings of God's majesty and goodness, and expresses complete faith in God's dominion. *Aleinu* and the Mourner's *Kaddish* conclude *Minḥah.*

## Shabbat Services

Shabbat, which begins at sundown Friday night, is devoted to prayer, study, the family, and rest. Shabbat services are longer than those on weekdays. *Maariv* on Friday evening is preceded by a brief special service of Welcoming Shabbat *(Kabbalat Shabbat).* This consists of six psalms and a liturgical poem, *Lekha Dodi,*

which was composed by a sixteenth-century mystic who person-
ified the Sabbath as a beloved bride. The poet lived in the city of
Safed, which is nestled in the Galilean hills of the Land of Israel,
then known as Palestine. Many mystics resided in Safed. It was
their custom to leave the city on Friday afternoon, dressed in
white, to welcome Queen Sabbath, and to usher her back as one
ushers in royalty. The author of *Lekha Dodi* urged his colleagues
(as indeed he urges all of us): "Come, my beloved, with chorus
of praise; Welcome Shabbat the Bride, Queen of our days."
Congregations generally sing this refrain in Hebrew, and some
of the poem's verses as well.

Before *Aleinu* on Friday night, *Kiddush* is recited over a cup
of wine. (*Kiddush,* like the word *Kaddish,* is related to the Hebrew word *kadosh,* which means "holy.") Traditionally, *Kiddush*
is recited at the table at home before the Sabbath meal. Since it
is such an important part of Shabbat observance, however, it is
recited during *Maariv* in case anybody at services for whatever
reason might be unable to chant the *Kiddush.* Chanting the words
of *Kiddush,* we proclaim the sanctity of the Sabbath and thank
God for the gift of the holy seventh day which commemorates
Creation and the Exodus from Egypt.

Something should be said here about the late Friday evening services conducted in most American congregations. Traditionally, men came to the synagogue late Friday afternoon for
*Minḥah, Kabbalat Shabbat,* and *Maariv.* They then went home to
their Shabbat meal and spent the evening quietly with their families. The principal Sabbath service was on Saturday morning.
This is still the practice in many communities. In the United
States, however, it was difficult for men to get to a Friday afternoon service before dusk. Stores could not be closed early, and
traveling took longer. The Reform movement replaced the traditional *Kabbalat Shabbat* and Sabbath *Maariv* with a late Friday
evening service for the entire family. This fulfilled a need on the
American scene, and many Conservative and Orthodox congregations have adopted this practice. Some congregations hold late

Friday evening services only during the fall, winter, and spring, but not in the summer. Since such services are of relatively recent origin, they do not follow a uniform pattern.

### Shabbat Shaḥarit

The Saturday morning service *(Shaḥarit)* also includes special features, including the addition of poetic passages extolling Creation and the joy and beauty of Shabbat. The middle *berakhah* of the *Amidah* is devoted to the theme of Shabbat.

### The Torah Service

In the absence of weekday routine, there is more time on Shabbat for the reading of the Torah and for the study of its sacred words. This is an important aspect of the spiritual regeneration of Shabbat.

The Torah consists of the Five Books of Moses: Genesis, Exodus, Leviticus, Numbers, and Deuteronomy. (In Hebrew each book is known by its first word, so you may hear them referred to respectively as *Bereshit, Sh'mot, Va-yikra, B'midbar,* and *D'varim.*)

The word *Torah* literally means "Instruction"; it was mistranslated into Greek as "Law." The Torah does contain laws, but it also includes ethical insights and demands, history, ritual, poetry, and prayer. It is a guide to authentic religious living. Most Jews believe that it was divinely revealed, though they differ over the definition of revelation. The Torah has been called the constitution of the Jewish people, for its teachings are the foundation of all Jewish life.

The Torah is not the whole Bible, although it is the most sacred of all biblical texts. The other books of the Bible are found in two groupings: the Prophets and the Writings. The first six books of Prophets—Joshua, Judges, Samuel I and II, and Kings I and II—tell the story of the Israelites from the time they entered the Promised Land under the leadership of Joshua in the thirteenth century B.C.E. until the Babylonians destroyed the First Kingdom in 586 B.C.E. The other books of this grouping contain the messages of those inspired men we think of when we say "prophet," including Amos, Hosea, Isaiah, Jeremiah, Ezekiel, and Micah.

The Writings contain the religious poetry of the Book of Psalms, the teachings about attitudes and conduct in the Book of Proverbs, the theological speculations of Job and Ecclesiastes, the sensuous poetry of the Song of Songs, and the sweet story of Ruth, as well as Lamentations, Jonah, Esther, Daniel, Ezra, Nehemiah, and Chronicles I and II.

Near the end of the *Shaharit* service the Torah Scroll *(Sefer Torah;* plural: *Sifrei Torah)* is removed from the special Ark where the Torah Scrolls are kept. The curtain *(parokhet)* is pulled back, the doors are parted, and the Torah is taken out. A formal procession through the congregation allows people to express love and respect for the Torah by kissing the mantle covering it. After the crown, breastplate, and mantle of the *Sefer Torah* are removed, the Torah Scroll is placed on a reading desk and opened to the place where the reading is to begin.

A different section (called *sidrah* or *parashah*) is read each week. It is the continuation of the verses which were read the previous Sabbath morning and is the same throughout the world in every synagogue which follows the annual cycle of readings. The Torah is divided into sections which allow for the complete reading of all five books each year. The cycle begins with the first words of the Book of Genesis each fall, after the holidays which initiate the new year of the Jewish calendar.

In ancient Palestine, it took three years to complete a reading of the entire Torah. In Babylonia, however, the reading was completed in one year. The Babylonian practice was adopted by all Jewish communities. In recent decades, however, some rabbis and their congregations have returned to the older triennial cycle. They have not reintroduced the precise form of the old Palestinian system, because they want to preserve the unity of Jewry's religious expression by reading from the same portion from which everyone else is reading. Therefore, they read one-third of the weekly *sidrah* (i.e., one-third of the portion read in its entirety by other congregations on the same morning). Each year, a different third of the weekly *sidrah* is read. Thus the entire Torah is completed every three years (hence the term *triennial cycle*).

Who reads the Torah in the synagogue? Anyone who has mastered the art. And indeed it is an art! The Torah Scroll does not contain a printed text. It is painstakingly written by hand on parchment by a scribe, who must follow the exact procedures used by his predecessors throughout the centuries. Modern Hebrew books may be printed with vowels. A Torah Scroll contains no vowels. Moreover, it contains no punctuation. Further, since the division of the Bible into verses and chapters did not exist before the Middle Ages, there are no verses or chapters indicated in the Torah Scroll. The Torah reader (called *baal korei*) must prepare most carefully in order to read correctly and to know where to pause or to stop.

Actually, the Torah is not read; it is chanted. Each word has a specific assigned cantillation, indicated in printed Bibles by certain markings called trope. The *baal korei* must learn the proper chant from a printed text and then transfer it mentally to the reading from the Torah Scroll. In most Reform congregations, it is customary for the Torah to be read, not chanted.

Each *sidrah* is divided into subsections, before and after which someone recites a blessing *(berakhah)* thanking God for the gift of the Torah. It is an honor to be asked to recite this blessing. This honor is known as an *aliyah* (literally, "a going up"). In most congregations, the first person called is a *kohen,* a descendant of the priests *(kohanim)* who functioned in the ancient Temple. The second *aliyah* is given to a *levi,* a descendant of the Levites who also served in the ancient Temple in Jerusalem. The remaining *aliyot* (plural of *aliyah*) are given to those who are in neither category. Each one of them is known as "Israelite" *(yisrael)*. On Shabbat, seven people are called to the Torah. On Festivals there are five *aliyot*. On *Rosh Ḥodesh* (first of the month) there are four. Each individual with an *aliyah* kisses the Torah Scroll with a *tallit* or some other appropriate object and recites the *berakhah*. Then the *baal korei* reads from the Torah, after which the honoree again kisses the Torah and recites a second *berakhah*.

There are three other occasions during the week when the Torah is read. A portion is read at Shabbat *Minḥah*. It consists of the beginning of the new section following the one read on Shabbat morning. The same brief portion is read at Morning Services on Monday and on Thursday. At these times, three people are honored with an *aliyah*.

On Shabbat and Festivals, an additional person is called for an *aliyah*: the *maftir* (which means "additional"). This portion usually is a repetition of the last few verses of the section read. On Festivals, a portion is read from a second *Sefer Torah*. Two more people are then called to the Torah. One (called *magbiah*) raises the Torah Scroll and sits with it, holding it in an upright position. The second (called *gollel*) ties a sash around the middle of the rolled Scroll and slips the mantle over it.

The *maftir* then chants a designated passage from one of the prophetic books of the Bible. This selection is called *haftarah*. It has some relationship to the *sidrah* or to the Festival Reading—a similarity of ideas or an association with a theme, personality, or specific words mentioned in the Torah Reading. The *haftarah* is ordinarily chanted from a printed text rather than from a scroll. The symbols indicating the proper melody for the *haftarah* are the same as those for the Torah Reading, yet they indicate different chants. Being asked to chant the *haftarah* is regarded as a great honor.

When the Torah Scroll is returned to the Ark, the congregation chants several passages, concluding with the singing of these words in Hebrew:

> It is a tree of life for those who grasp it, and all who uphold it are blessed. Its ways are pleasantness, and all its paths are peace.

Help us turn to You, and we shall return. Renew our lives as in
days of old.

The Ark is then closed.

At this point, there may be a sermon or an explanation of
the Torah portion. The sermon is not as important in Jewish as
in Protestant services. For centuries, sermons were rarely delivered on Shabbat morning. The rabbi would on occasion deliver
a learned discourse, but the kind of address we associate with the
word sermon was given in the afternoon by an itinerant preacher
*(magid)* who specialized in homiletics. In the United States,
however, it has become customary for the rabbi to give sermons
each week. Some preach only on Friday night, reserving Shabbat
morning for teaching the Torah portion or *haftarah*.

### The Musaf Service

*Musaf* means "addition" or "supplement." It is a term for the additional sacrifice offered on the Sabbath and on Festivals in the
ancient Temple (in addition to the sacrifice offered every day). A
*Musaf* service is also added after *Shaḥarit* on the first morning of
each month in the Hebrew calendar, which is lunar. That day,
*Rosh Ḥodesh,* was once observed as a semiholiday on which
women especially were relieved of routine household chores.

*Musaf* begins with an *Amidah* whose middle *berakhah* includes a petition for the restoration of the ritual of animal sacrifice as in the ancient Temple service. Many Jews who do not wish
for a return to animal sacrifice find other implications in *Musaf,*
including the expression of their love and yearning for Zion. They
have modified the middle *berakhah* so that it articulates reverence
for our ancestors' mode of worship without asking for a return
to that worship through animal sacrifice. The Conservative Siddur, for example, changed the conventional prayer, which reads:
"May it be Thy will, O Lord our God and God of our fathers,
to lead us up in joy to our land, and to plant us within its bor-

ders, where we will offer up unto Thee the sacrifices that we are obliged to offer. . . ." It now reads, "May it be Your will, O Lord our God and God of our fathers, to lead us joyfully back to our land, and to establish us within its borders where our forefathers prepared their daily offerings and the additional Sabbath offerings. . . ."

After the *Musaf Amidah,* the congregation sings one of the most popular liturgical poems: *Ein Keloheinu.* It proclaims the uniqueness of God, asserting that there is none like our God, our Lord, our King, our Deliverer. This hymn is followed by *Aleinu,* the Mourner's *Kaddish,* and usually the hymn *Adon Olam.*

### Shabbat Minḥah

Shabbat *Minḥah* includes a short reading from the Torah and features a distinctive chanting of the liturgy, which differs from that of all other services.

### The Congregation

According to Jewish law, Jews can pray anywhere, as individuals or as members of a congregation, though services as we know them by and large take place in a synagogue.

A congregation may be formed by any group of ten or more Jewish adults. Traditionally, the ten have had to be males. (The requirement for ten is based upon a passage in the Torah which refers to ten men as constituting a "congregation.") This is still so in all Orthodox and in many Conservative congregations. Some of these allow groups of women to organize and conduct their own services. In 1973, the Committee on Jewish Law and Standards of the Rabbinical Assembly ruled that women may be counted as part of the required quorum *(minyan)*. Some Conservative congregations follow that ruling. Reform authorities have eliminated the numerical minimum as a requirement for congregational worship.

Since the Hebrew word for "number" is *minyan,* the service itself, participated in by a minimum number of ten, is commonly referred to as "the *minyan.*" At a synagogue, one often hears such remarks as "we need one more for a *minyan*" or "we have a *minyan* now."

Some passages in the prayerbook may be recited only in the presence of a *minyan.* These include the formal call to worship (known as *Barkhu*) in the morning and the evening services. The *Kaddish,* in any of its forms, is another such passage.

The *Amidah* is included in each of the three daily services. Because some members of the congregation were unable to read the words of Hebrew prayer, rabbinic authorities introduced the practice of having a leader chant the words of the *Amidah* aloud at the conclusion of the silent recitation. In the absence of a *minyan,* however, the *Amidah* is not repeated aloud. (And the *Amidah* is never repeated at the evening services.)

Jews as individuals or as part of a congregation may pray anywhere, may fulfill religious obligations even if there is no synagogue in a community. Conversely, faithful attendance at synagogue services does not automatically confer special religious status. A pious Jew has many religious duties outside the synagogue.

Although Jews do not need a synagogue in order to be religious, they have always regarded it as more meritorious to commune with God together with others than as individuals. People often find strength and inspiration from praying at fixed times with other Jews who share the faith and the tradition. A purpose of congregational prayer is to provide a framework for increasingly higher levels of religiosity.

## The Synagogue

Jews traditionally have organized themselves into congregations that are larger than one *minyan.* Over time they usually have chosen a rabbi to provide regular leadership and to teach them. They have located rooms or built buildings in which to worship, furnishing and decorating them according to their own sense of aesthetics. To meet their religious and communal needs, they created the institution known as the synagogue. The character of each congregation depends on the size and personality of its membership.

The rabbi is the congregation's authority in all religious matters. Having earned the title after years of difficult study, culminating in ordination, the rabbi is an authority on interpreting and deciding matters of Jewish law and practice.

In contemporary America, the rabbi in most congregations preaches weekly sermons, teaches on many levels within the congregation and the general community, counsels congregants, leads communal activities, and oversees matters of synagogue administration, in addition to leading services.

In recent years, pressure has mounted for the ordination of women as rabbis. The Reform, Reconstructionist, and Conservative rabbinical schools do ordain women. Orthodox authorities do not consider the possibility of women rabbis. Although the number of women rabbis is presently small, it undoubtedly will grow in the years to come.

Each congregation selects its own rabbi, turning to the national body with which it is affiliated for acceptable candidates. The recommended candidates are interviewed by a congregational committee which makes a recommendation to be acted upon by the membership who have the authority to elect a rabbi.

A congregation often chooses another religious leader: the *ḥazzan,* or cantor, whose area of expertise is music. There is an elaborate musical tradition associated with the liturgy of the synagogue. The *ḥazzan* chants the service, is responsible for all of its musical aspects, and often serves as teacher and as a musical resource within the community. Although congregations are free to elect anyone without formal training to the position of *ḥaz-*

*zan,* contemporary synagogues have increasingly required that cantors be professionally trained at recognized institutions. Cantorial schools have been established to provide professional training. (A few congregations have begun to accept female cantors.)

Another member of the synagogue staff may be a *shamash.* This word is usually translated "sexton." The *shamash* is not a custodian. His responsibilities usually include all arrangements in connection with daily services and various ritual details in the life of the congregation. The *shamash* may be expected to serve as Torah Reader, to lead some of the services, and to teach some classes for children or adults.

The synagogue is a uniquely Jewish institution. It may share certain functions with the church, but it is not a "Jewish church." The church is an offspring of the synagogue, but its main functions were defined by the nature of Christianity after it broke away from Judaism. The church is essentially a place of worship. It may house other activities, particularly in contemporary America, but its extracurricular activities are secondary to its main function as a house of worship. Because Christians are a faith community rather than a people, they often focus on the individual's spiritual needs rather than on communal needs.

The synagogue is classically a house of assembly *(bet k'nesset)* and a house of study *(bet midrash)* as well as a house of worship *(bet tefillah).* Jews turn to the synagogue for educational and social needs as well as purely spiritual ones.

The word "synagogue" is used by all Jewish communities, but in the United States the word "temple" is sometimes substituted. When the early Reform movement rejected the traditional prayer for the rebuilding of the Temple in Jerusalem and declared contemporary houses of worship to be its equivalent, they began referring to the latter as temples. Orthodox and Conservative Jews, although retaining that prayer as part of their anticipation of a restored Zion, have called some synagogues temples as well.

The Yiddish word for synagogue is *shul.* It is derived from the word for school, reflecting the fact that education has always been a basic function of the synagogue.

There is no standard synagogue architecture. Structures vary from community to community and within the same community. Synagogue architecture traditionally has been influenced by the architecture of its environment. Yet there are certain features common to all synagogues. In the center of the wall facing the congregants (usually the eastern wall) is an Ark *(Aron Kodesh)* containing at least one Torah Scroll (usually a number of Scrolls). The quantity is often related to the affluence of the congregation. There are occasions when it is necessary during a service to read from two or three different books of the Torah, and it is easier to do so from different scrolls prepared in advance than to require the congregation to wait while a single Scroll is rolled.

The parchment Scroll is covered by a mantle of velvet or silk. Often it is adorned with a crown, symbolizing the sovereignty of Torah in Jewish life. Most Torah mantles are adorned with silver breastplates. A pointer, used when the Torah is read, usually hangs near the breastplate.

Above the Ark is an Eternal Light *(Ner Tamid)*. It also symbolizes the eternal truth of the Torah.

In most Western synagogues the Ark is on a raised platform resembling a stage. This is referred to as "the pulpit" or *bimah*. Traditionally, the *bimah* was in the center of the synagogue away from the Ark. The Torah was read from that *bimah*. In contemporary synagogues, chairs are placed on the pulpit on either side of the Ark. They have no special significance other than being considered seats of honor. They are occupied by the rabbi, the cantor, the president of the congregation, and anyone else invited to sit there.

Traditionally, no instrumental music was used in the service, although instruments were used in the ancient Temple. As a sign of mourning for the Temple's destruction, musical instruments were not employed in the synagogue service. The traditional synagogue had no organ loft, no choir loft. When a choir was used, the singers simply sat on the *bimah* or stood near the center. Most Reform congregations and some Conservative congregations today have introduced the organ and choral music into the service.

Whatever other symbols may be found in a particular synagogue have been chosen by the builders. In some congregations, a *menorah* (candelabrum) is placed on or near the pulpit. It is not required by Jewish law. Very often, two tablets representing the tablets of the Ten Commandments are placed above the Ark. Sometimes the figure of a lion, the symbol of Judah, is placed alongside each tablet. Scriptural verses or rabbinic statements often adorn the Ark. One of the most popular, taken from the Talmud, is: "Know before whom you stand."

## Suggested Readings for Further Study

Donin, Haim Halevy, *To Pray as a Jew* (New York: Basic Books, 1980)

Garfiel, Evelyn, *The Service of the Heart* (North Hollywood: Wilshire Books Company, 1958)

Millgram, Abraham, *Jewish Worship* (Philadelphia: The Jewish Publication Society, 1973)

ADDITIONAL SUGGESTIONS

De Breffny, Brian, *The Synagogue* (New York: MacMillan Publishing Company, 1979)

Heschel, Abraham Joshua, *Man's Quest for God* (New York): Charles Scribner's Sons, 1954)

Kaploun, Uri, editor, *The Synagogue* (Philadelphia: The Jewish Publication Society, 1973)

Martin, Bernard, *Prayer in Judaism* (New York and London: Basic Books, 1968)

Petuchowski, Jacob, editor, *Understanding Jewish Prayer* (New York: KTAV Publishing House, 1972)

Rossel, Seymour, *When a Jew Prays* (New York: Behrman House, 1973)

## *Prayerbooks*

Birnbaum, Philip, editor, *Daily Prayer Book* (New York: Hebrew Publishing Company, 1949)

Bokser, Ben Zion, editor, *The Prayer Book* (New York: Hebrew Publishing Company, 1957)

———, *High Holy Day Prayer Book* (New York: Hebrew Publishing Company, 1959)

Harlow, Jules, editor, *Mahzor for Rosh Hashanah and Yom Kippur* (New York: The Rabbinical Assembly, 1972)

———, *Siddur Sim Shalom* (New York: The Rabbinical Assembly and The United Synagogue of America, 1985)

Hertz, Joseph H., editor, *The Prayer Book* (New York: Bloch Publishing Company, 1948)

Pool, David de Sola, editor, *The Traditional Prayer Book* (New York: Behrman House and The Rabbinical Council of America, 1960)

Silverman, Morris, editor, *Sabbath and Festival Prayerbook* (New York: The Rabbinical Assembly and The United Synagogue of America, 1946)

Stern, Chaim, editor, *Gates of Prayer* (Cincinnati: The Central Conference of American Rabbis, 1975)

CHAPTER 5

# Holy Days and Festivals

*A*SIDE from Shabbat, the most important days of the Jewish calendar are *Rosh Hashanah* and *Yom Kippur, Sukkot, Pe-sah,* and *Shavuot.* Their recurring cycle gives the year spiritual meaning and ritual texture. Each is known as a *yom tov* in He-brew, a *yontiff* in Yiddish. You will often hear Jews whose fam-ilies came from Europe saying *goot yontiff* to each other on these days. The Hebrew *yom tov* is often translated as "holiday", but its meaning is really "holy day." (Literally it means a "good day".)

Each *yom tov* is observed one day by Reform Jews and two days by others. (*Yom Kippur* is observed one day by all.) The two-day observances date from the time before a fixed calendar was established. People living far from Jerusalem could never be cer-tain about the exact date of a *yom tov* because communications were so poor. They observed the *yom tov* for two days to make sure they were observing one on the correct date. This practice became a fixed tradition outside the Holy Land and continues today everywhere but in Israel. Reform Jews, and some congre-gations in the Conservative and Reconstructionist movements, believe that the rebirth of the Jewish State in the Land of Israel signals the end of the necessity to observe the second day, although all Conservative and some Reform congregations observe *Rosh Hashanah* for two days.

## The High Holy Days

The religious cycle of the year begins with *Rosh Hashanah* (literally, "head of the year") and *Yom Kippur,* the Day of Atonement. They are often called the High Holy Days or The Days of Awe. *Rosh Hashanah* is also known as the Day of Judgment. These Holy Days and the days between them are known as the Days of Repentance.

*Rosh Hashanah* and *Yom Kippur* are days set aside wholly for the spirit. They do not commemorate a specific historical event or any cyclical change in nature. They are devoted to critical self-examination, introspection, and spiritual stocktaking. On these days Jews are expected to ponder carefully their conduct of the past year, to acknowledge their faults and sins, to repent of them, to ask forgiveness of those who have been offended, and to resolve not to repeat the sins. Repentance, though, is not simply a ritual act which wipes the slate clean. The Hebrew word for repentance *(teshuvah)* means "return." It implies returning to the point where one went astray and then proceeding on a new path which avoids the errors of the old. It connotes a return to God and to God's ways.

The themes of *Rosh Hashanah* liturgy deal with judgment, our allegiance to God, and the meaning of life. The quality of our life may well be determined by the ideas, inspirations, and decisions reached or reaffirmed during these days. Judaism teaches that all of us have the power to choose good and reject evil. Even though the liturgy declares that our destiny is determined by our previous conduct, it also states that it can always be altered by repentance, prayer, and moral living.

One of the few ritual obligations of *Rosh Hashanah* is to listen to the *shofar,* the sound of the ram's horn. There are several reasons why this primitive instrument is sounded during the Days of Awe. A ram's horn is mentioned in the Book of Genesis, in the narrative known as the Binding of Isaac, which is the Torah Reading for the second day of *Rosh Hashanah.* The Patriarch Abraham, at God's command, bound his son Isaac upon an altar on a mountaintop, prior to offering him as a sacrifice. Abraham was stopped at the last moment by an angel of God and commanded to substitute a ram for Isaac. The ram's horn recalls for each of us the intense faith of the first Hebrew.

The *shofar* was sounded in ancient times at the coronation of kings. On the High Holy Days we proclaim our faith that no human being or human institution is supreme, that God alone is our Sovereign.

The *shofar,* sounded at Mount Sinai when the Ten Commandments were given, calls us to renew our dedication to the moral law. Tradition has it that the *shofar* will be sounded to announce the advent of the Messianic age. The *shofar* is also a call to arouse us from moral lethargy. Maimonides declared:

> The shofar exclaims: Wake up from your slumber! Examine your deeds, and turn in repentance, remembering your Creator. You sleepers who forget the truth while caught up in the fads and follies of the time, frittering away your years in vanity and emptiness which cannot help: take a good look at yourselves. Improve your ways. Let everyone abandon his bad deeds and his wicked thoughts.

The High Holy Days are ushered in at home with the recitation of special *berakhot* as the candles are lit on the evenings of Rosh Hashanah. At the dinner table, as on Shabbat, *hamotzi* is recited over *hallah* and *kiddush* is chanted over wine. At *Rosh Hashanah* it is traditional to use a round rather than a braided *hallah,* symbolizing the completion of one year and the beginning of another. It is customary for those at the table to dip sliced apples in honey while wishing each other a sweet new year. Many people send New Year greetings to relatives and friends.

An interesting custom practiced on the afternoon of the first day of *Rosh Hashanah* is called *Tashlikh*. If the first day is on Shabbat, *Tashlikh* takes place on the second day. The word *tashlikh* is found in a verse in the Book of Micah (7:19): "You will cast *(tashlikh)* all our sins into the depths of the sea." We symbolically cast our sins into a sea, river, stream, or any other body of water. At the edge of the water, the verse from Micah and other passages are recited, and crumbs are taken out of pockets and cast into the water as a symbolic statement that we can remove sin from our lives.

We often are more aware of physical desires than of spiritual needs. Physical desires also seem to be more easily satisfied. *Yom Kippur* emphasizes proper priorities. By not eating or drinking, by not satisfying physical demands, we focus on the importance of the spiritual dimension of our life.

*Yom Kippur* begins with an evening service. People gather for the last prefast meal in the late afternoon in order to arrive at the synagogue before the chanting of *Kol Nidrei,* which begins before sundown. At home, many people light a *yahrzeit* candle which burns for 24 hours in memory of a relative or other loved one. *Kol Nidrei* is a moving liturgical highlight of the year, although it is not actually a prayer. It is a legal formula which emphasizes that all the words which we utter are serious commitments. The formula releases worshipers from promises made to God that they might not fulfill, removing the guilt of unfulfilled commitments. The formula cannot absolve us of vows made to other human beings. The traditional chant and its associations are deeply moving. The chant seems to convey the essence of Yom Kippur. Many people speak of *Yom Kippur* evening as *Kol Nidrei* Eve.

The entire next day is spent in the synagogue. The prayerbook marks four distinct services, but the congregation regards them as one, daylong service. The liturgy states and elaborates upon the subjects that are of prime concern on *Yom Kippur*: sin, forgiveness, atonement. It describes the manner in which *Yom Kippur* was observed in the ancient Temple. Five times on *Yom Kippur* the congregation rises to ask forgiveness for a variety of sins, accepting the concept of corporate responsibility. As Professor Abraham Joshua Heschel pointed out, only some are guilty of each sin, but all are responsible. The Confession is not couched in the singular ("I have sinned") but in the plural ("We have sinned"). Together we recognize the evil of immoral acts, together we seek to atone for them. The Book of Jonah is chanted as the *Haftarah* during the afternoon Torah Service. It emphasizes God's compassion for all creatures.

The awesome day comes to a close as the sun sets. The final service of *N'eelah* (literally "closing"), is followed by a final sounding of the *shofar*. A weekday *Maariv* service and a *havdalah* ceremony conclude the long day.

After services, family and friends gather to break the fast together.

### The Pilgrimage Festivals

In the Torah it is written that God commanded the Jews to appear before Him on Passover, *Shavuot,* and *Sukkot*. In ancient times, Jews went on pilgrimages up to the Temple in Jerusalem with their offerings. Since the year 70 C.E. there has been no Temple in Jerusalem, but the term "Pilgrimage Festivals" has been retained for these three holidays. Many contemporary Jews honor the concept by visiting Jerusalem during one of the Festivals at least once, if not annually.

SUKKOT

Five days after the intensely spiritual, introspective and triumphant close of *Yom Kippur, Sukkot* begins. It is the great festival of thanksgiving. Many begin building their *sukkah,* a temporary shelter, right after the close of *Yom Kippur* services. *Sukkot* lasts eight days. The first two and last two have the status of holy days with special synagogue services. On the other days, known as "intermediate days" *(ḥol ha-mo'ed)*, there are special additions to the weekday service but normal work patterns are permitted.

Many *Sukkot* observances remind us of how much we have to be thankful for. The focus of observance is the *sukkah,* a temporary room that is built next to the home or synagogue, ranging from the simple to the elaborate. The *sukkah* has walls but no roof. Green boughs attached to the rafters serve as the roof, through which the stars should be visible. People hang fruits and vegetables from the top and on the walls of the *sukkah* to symbolize the bounty of the harvest and to remind us of our gratitude to God for creation and sustenance. Some families eat all their meals in the *sukkah.* The very pious spend as much time as possible in the *sukkah*; some even sleep there. People without their own *sukkah* go to a neighbor's or to the synagogue's for *kiddush* in order to fulfill the commandment to say the special *berakhot* and to eat some food in the *sukkah.*

The *sukkah* recalls the temporary shelters that the Israelites lived in on their wilderness journey from the slavery of Egypt toward the freedom of the Promised Land. It symbolizes the insecurity of the Jews throughout history, and of life itself, as well as the triumph of spiritual power over physical suffering.

In the synagogue on every day of *Sukkot* except for Shabbat, people hold a palm branch *(lulav)* and a citron *(etrog)* at one point in the service, and recite blessings over them. The palm is the most majestic tree in the Middle East. The citron is a lemonlike fruit with a lovely aroma. The *lulav* is bound together with three myrtle branches and two willow branches. The fruit and the branches represent the bounty of the earth.

As you would expect, the liturgy reflects the emphasis on thanksgiving. On *Sukkot,* as on every Festival, psalms known liturgically as *Hallel* are added to the service. *Lulav* and *etrog* (plural: *lulavim* and *etrogim*) are held while *Hallel* is chanted. Special *Sukkot* prayers called *Hoshanot* are recited as members of the congregation march around the synagogue in a procession while holding their *lulavim* and *etrogim*. As on other Festivals, five people are called up to the Torah. It is customary to read the Book of Ecclesiastes during this holiday.

The eighth day of *Sukkot* is distinct. It is called *Sh'mini Atze-ret* (the Eighth Day of Assembly). People stop using their *lulavim* and *etrogim,* and no longer eat in the *sukkah*. A distinguishing feature of the service is *Yizkor,* the memorial service which is also recited on Passover, *Shavuot,* and *Yom Kippur*.

For the past thousand years, Jews have celebrated another *yom tov* at the end of the week of Sukkot. *Simḥat Torah* (Rejoicing over the Torah) is the day on which the reading of the Torah is completed and its rereading is begun. The synagogue reverberates with exuberance. During both the evening and morning services all the Torah Scrolls which the synagogue owns are carried in a festive procession throughout the sanctuary. People sing and dance in the aisles. Every man and, in many congregations, every woman is given the opportunity to carry a Torah Scroll. Children follow in the parade with flags that are sometimes topped with apples.

At the morning service everyone, including each child, receives the honor of being called to the Torah. The two greatest honors are reserved for the individuals who are called before the last verses of Deuteronomy and before the first verses of Genesis are read.

Those congregations which no longer observe the second day of *yom tov* follow the Israeli practice of combining *Sh'mini Atze-ret* and *Simḥat Torah* on one day.

## PASSOVER

As *Sukkot* celebrates the Fall harvest, Passover celebrates Spring. As *Sukkot* recalls the journey through the desert, Passover recalls the redemption from Egypt. Passover is the great Festival of Freedom. It obliges each of us to consider himself or herself as personally having been redeemed from bondage. In commemorating the Exodus of the Israelites from slavery, Passover teaches that the God of Israel wants all people to be free. Because the Exodus marked the transition of the Jews from a family of tribes to a people, Passover celebrates the birth of a nation.

The festival is marked by a strict prohibition (found in the Torah) against eating leavened bread or any foods with ingredients that might contain leavening. Passover preparations begin with a thorough housecleaning to rid the home of any trace of leavening (*ḥametz*). *Matzah,* unleavened bread, is also known as the bread of affliction. It should remind us of our ancestors' hardships in Egyptian slavery, as well as the haste of their departure.

Before Passover, observant Jews clean out closets, reline shelves, and store the cookware and dishes they use during the rest of the year. Then they bring out the special Passover dishes, silverware, and pots and pans. Metal, and glass dishes used throughout the year can be kashered for *Pesaḥ*. For many people, these preparations heighten the anticipation of the *yom tov*.

Any foods considered *ḥametz* are sealed away in a closet. Many follow the custom of giving unopened boxes and cans of food to the non-Jewish poor. Ashkenazic Jews consider rice and legumes to be *ḥametz*; Sephardic Jews do not. Packaged goods must be certified as permissible for consumption on Passover.

The most important feature of Passover is the home service known as the *Seder*. The *Seder* includes a festive dinner, but it is much more than a banquet. The family and invited quests seated at the table participate in a religious service, using a special text called the *Haggadah,* of which there are countless editions. Usually one person leads the others in reading and chanting the *Haggadah,* which includes a running narration whose focus is the story of the Exodus, with commentaries, prayers and folk songs. Everyone is free to raise questions and to participate in suggesting answers, to explore the meaning of freedom in their own lives and in the lives of others. There is a prescribed order *(seder)* for all of the text and rituals, which precede and follow the meal.

A basic function of the *Seder* is to transmit the meaning of the Exodus and the theme of freedom to the next generation. Children are encouraged to participate actively in the *Seder*. Some editions of the *Haggadah* include supplementary texts which highlight the significance of Passover for the contemporary Jew.

In the synagogue service, the Torah readings and *haftarah* readings are related to the holiday, as they are during each Festival. Five people are called to the Torah. The middle blessing of the *Amidah* reflects the Passover Festival. Psalms of praise (known as *Hallel*) are sung. It is customary to read the Song of Songs during this holiday.

SHAVUOT

*Shavuot,* meaning "weeks," follows Passover by seven weeks. In English it is called Pentecost, since it comes fifty days after Passover.

According to tradition, there were seven weeks between the Exodus from Egypt and God's giving the Torah at Mount Sinai. For many observant Jews, the time between the two festivals of Passover and *Shavuot* is one of increasing spiritual intensity. In recent years, an increasing number of people have been reviving the tradition of studying biblical and rabbinic texts throughout the first night of *Shavuot,* as a way of celebrating the Revelation of Torah commemorated by the Festival. This special period of study is known as a *tikkun,* or *tikkun leil Shavuot.*

*Shavuot* is also associated with the harvest, coming at the end of spring. In ancient times Israelites brought an offering of the first fruits from their harvest to the Temple in Jerusalem. During the centuries of exile from the Land of Israel, when Jews were rarely allowed to own land or to practice agriculture, this aspect of *Shavuot* remained only a memory. In Israel today, however, Jews have renewed their love for the soil and agriculture. They have revived the ceremony of first fruits. Many kibbutzim, even the nonobservant ones, commemorate *Shavuot* as an agricultural festival.

Unlike Passover, *Shavuot* has no specific home ritual associated with it, although it is customary among Jews of European
ancestry to each cheese blintzes and other dairy foods on *Shavuot*. Synagogue services are similar to those for the other two
Festivals, with a major difference: on *Shavuot* it is customary to
read the Book of Ruth. Ruth, born a Moabite, chose to become
part of the Jewish people and to accept their Torah as her own,
just as the Jews accepted the Torah at Mount Sinai.

## Special Days

### HANUKKAH

The holiday of Ḥanukkah follows *Sukkot* by eight and a half
weeks, usually in the month of December. It bears no relationship to Christmas beyond the fact that it is celebrated during the
same season. In the middle of the second pre-Christian century,
the Greek ruler of Palestine (King Antiochus of Syria) sought to
impose the Greek religion and the Greek way of life upon the
Jews. His troops converted the Temple in Jerusalem into a Temple of Zeus.

In 167 B.C.E., a small group of Jews rose in revolt. They were
led by members of the Hasmonean family, whose distinguished
leader was Judah the Maccabee. After three years of guerrilla
warfare they overcame the more numerous and powerful foe. In
164 B.C.E., they recaptured Jerusalem, cleansed the Temple, relit the
*menorah* (candelabrum) with ritually pure oil, and rededicated the
Temple. The Hebrew word for dedication is *ḥanukkah*. The
Maccabean battle was the first in history for religious freedom.
Their victory is celebrated as a triumph of the spirit. It should be
emphasized that Ḥanukkah also celebrates the victory of the
committed Jews over the assimilationists within the Jewish community, called Hellenists, who had adopted Greek attitudes and
customs.

Ḥanukkah is celebrated much more at home than in the
synagogue. Each evening, we light candles which are placed in a

*menorah*. On the first night, one candle is lit and appropriate *be-rakhot* are recited. One candle is added each night, leading to a total of eight candles on the eighth night. Songs, games, and the exchange of gifts may follow the candlelighting. Some people emphasize the gift giving, while other families deemphasize the gifts. Whatever people feel about gifts, they find Ḥanukkah a wonderful occasion for parties. Potato pancakes, or *latkes,* are featured on the menu. A favorite game involves spinning a special top called a *dreydl*. Traditionally the *menorah* is placed in a window, so that the light of the candles will publicly proclaim the celebration of the miracle.

PURIM

Purim follows Ḥanukkah by about two months. It also celebrates a victory over a powerful ruler who sought to destroy Jews and their way of life. The biblical Book of Esther records the story of an arch anti-Semite, Haman, prime minister of the Persian Empire, who planned to kill all the Jews in the empire. Queen Esther and her wise cousin Mordecai outwitted Haman. The king ordered that the Jews be protected and that Haman be hanged on the very day he had designated for their massacre.

Having experienced many Hamans throughout history, Jews have always taken courage from this story. Though anti-Semites have caused unimaginable pain, they have never succeeded in accomplishing their goal. Each of them has disappeared while the Jewish people continues to live.

Purim is among the happiest Jewish holidays. The synagogue celebration features a festive reading of the Book of Esther from a special scroll, called a *megillah*. Whenever the reader of the *megillah* pronounces the name of Haman, everyone responds with his or her favorite noisemaker *(grogger)* to drown out the name of one who sought to destroy us.

Purim is celebrated at home and in the community. Children and adults make fanciful costumes to wear at Purim parties as well as at the synagogue service. In Israel, gala parades with floats fill the streets. The menu for Purim features a three-cornered pastry filled with sweetened poppy seeds or with fruit. This pastry is known as *hamentaschen* (Haman's hat). It is traditional to deliver small packages of sweets, baked goods, and fruit *(mishloah manot)* to friends and neighbors. Purim is also a traditional time for collecting and distributing charity.

### TISHA B'AV

*Tisha B'Av* is the ninth (*tisha* means "nine") day in the Hebrew month of *Av,* occurring in the middle of the summer. Many calamities have befallen the Jewish people on this date throughout history. It is the anniversary of the destruction of both Temples in ancient Jerusalem (in 586 B.C.E. and 70 C.E.). On this date, other communities have been destroyed, and the Jews were expelled from Spain (in 1492). This sad anniversary is marked by a fast. Jews gather in the synagogue to listen to the reading of the Book of Lamentations and to chant sorrow-filled liturgical poems.

### TU BISHVAT

One month before Purim we observe *Tu Bishvat* ("the fifteenth day in the month of *Shevat*"). This is Jewish Arbor Day, the time when spring begins in the Holy Land with the first blossoming of trees. Because of their intense love for Zion, Jews have marked this day wherever they have lived by eating fruits associated with the Holy Land (citrus fruits, almonds or other nuts, figs, and carob.) With the birth of Zionism and the remarkable reforestation of the denuded land, *Tu Bishvat* has also become a day for encouraging the planting of trees in the Land of Israel. People can purchase trees to honor someone through the Jewish National Fund. They make a special effort to do so on *Tu Bishvat*.

### YOM HA-ATZMAUT (ISRAEL INDEPENDENCE DAY)

Since 1948, a new holiday has been added to the Jewish calendar. For centuries Jews prayed daily for the restoration of Zion, when they would again be a free people in their own land. Whatever the establishment of Israel may have meant as a haven of refuge, whatever its political significance may have been, it was also a triumph of a religious faith maintained throughout more than 1900 years of suffering and persecution. Therefore, whatever their citizenship and their political loyalties, many Jews regard Israel's birth as a great religious miracle. The day is marked in many synagogues by the recitation of the *Hallel* psalms of praise which are recited on *yom tov*. The Conservative movement has introduced an appropriate liturgical passage in the *Amidah* and in the *Blessings after Meals*. In Israel, the religious kibbutz movement has added a similar prayer. A Torah reading and a *haftarah* have also been designated for *Yom Ha-atzmaut*.

### YOM HA-SHOAH (REMEMBERING THE HOLOCAUST)

This day is set aside for remembering those whose lives were destroyed by Hitler and his followers. The anniversary of the final destruction of the Warsaw Ghetto, five days after Passover (the twenty-seventh of *Nissan*), has been chosen as the day when Jews the world over mourn and remember.

## Suggested Readings for Further Study

Goodman, Philip, *The Passover Anthology* (Philadelphia: The Jewish Publication Society, 1961)

———, *The Rosh Hashanah Anthology* (Philadelphia: The Jewish Publication Society, 1970)

———, *The Yom Kippur Anthology* (Philadelphia: The Jewish Publication Society, 1971)

Strassfeld, Michael, *The Jewish Holidays* (New York: Harper & Row, 1985)

Trepp, Leo, *The Complete Book of Jewish Observance* (New York: Behrman House/Summit Books, 1980)

# CHAPTER 6

# *Judaism: A Way of Living*

W E have begun to study Jewish prayer and to learn about the synagogue as a house of prayer, study, and assembly. Though the synagogue has been crucial for the survival of Judaism since the destruction of the Temple, the precepts of Jewish tradition are to be practiced as devotedly outside the synagogue as within its walls. Jewish tradition presents a system of ritual practice and moral behavior which are to be incorporated into the daily lives of its adherents.

To begin to understand the Jewish way of life, you should become familiar with one of the legal codes. The authoritative work of the sixteenth century, Rabbi Joseph Caro's *Shulḥan Arukh,* is the basis of all subsequent Jewish law, and is based upon discussions and decisions in ancient and medieval rabbinic literature as well as biblical passages. It spells out in detail the ritual and ethical demands placed upon the individual in all aspects of life. It is not possible to summarize adequately the *Shulḥan Arukh* or any other code here. We can only begin to present an understanding of what Jewish conduct should be. Contemporary Orthodox and Conservative authorities may differ in how they apply the *Shulḥan Arukh* to modern Jewish life, but all recognize it as the basis for their decisions.

A basic concept which informs all of Jewish law and practice must constantly be kept in mind. It is found in the nineteenth chapter of the Book of Leviticus: "You shall be holy, for I, the Lord your God, am holy." Jewish tradition maintains that a holy life is an attainable goal for every individual. The details of Jewish practice can lead us to that goal.

## Elements of Daily Life

### PRAYER

For observant Jews, the day begins and ends with prayer. They may not always go to the synagogue for morning, afternoon, or evening services, but they recite the morning, afternoon, and evening prayers at home and even away from home. Adult males are expected to wear *tzitzit* and to put on *tefillin* every morning except Shabbat, holidays, and *Tisha B'av*.

The Hebrew word *tzitzit* (pronounced *tzitzis* in Ashkenazic Hebrew) means fringes. We see them most often at the corners of the prayer shawl *(tallit)*. The commandment to wear *tzitzit* is found in Numbers 15:37–39. (For a translation, see page 40.) One of those verses explains the purpose concisely: "Looking upon these fringes you will be reminded of all the commandments of the Lord and fulfill them, and not be seduced by your heart or led astray by your eyes."

Very observant people have interpreted the biblical command to mean that they should wear fringes all day. Since wearing a *tallit* all day would be awkward, they wear a small *tallit (tallit katan)* under the shirt. It is a square cloth with an opening for the head, with *tzitzit* attached at the corners. Some people allow the *tzitzit* to show. The prayer shawl is worn only at morning services and on the eve of *Yom Kippur, Kol Nidre* night, when it is put on before nightfall.

An observant Jew also puts on *tefillin* at morning prayers. *Tefillin* consist of two small leather boxes with attached leather thongs. One box is placed on the left arm (unless the person is left-handed, when it is placed on the right) and tightened just above the elbow. The single thong is then wound around the forearm seven times. The other box is placed upon the head, with one of its attached thongs falling to the left and the other to the right. Next, the thong on the arm is wrapped around the fingers in a prescribed way. The boxes contain small parchment scrolls on which a scribe has written verses from Exodus 13:1–10, 11:16 and from Deuteronomy 6:4–9, 11:13–21. These passages, in the words of the prayerbook, "teach the unity of God, recall the miracle of the Exodus, declare His dominion over all that is in the heavens and on earth, and affirm our duty to serve God with soul and heart and mind." One of the verses from Deuteronomy is understood to refer to *tefillin*: "You shall bind them (words of Torah) as a sign upon your hand, they shall be a symbol above your eyes . . ."

Traditionally, women have not worn a *tallit* or put on *tefillin*. Some women, however, are beginning to take this obligation upon themselves.

A Jewish home is distinguished in a number of ways, one of which begins at the entrance. The *mezuzah* is a small case attached to the doorway of the home. Each *mezuzah* contains a piece of parchment on which a scribe has written the verses of Deuteronomy 6:4–9. (For a translation, see page 39.) It includes the verse which declares "you shall inscribe them (words of Torah) upon the doorposts of your homes and upon your gates." The *mezuzah* is a constant reminder of the values which should inform the behavior of those who enter the doors of the home to which it is attached.

A *mezuzah* should also be attached to the doorway of every room in the house, except the bathroom. It is attached to the doorway diagonally with the top leaning toward the inside and the bottom toward the outside. It is placed on the upper third of the doorpost, on the right side as one enters.

KASHRUT

Dietary laws *(kashrut)* constitute a discipline which elevates satisfying the appetite into a religious act. Those who accept this discipline are spoken of as people who "keep *kosher*." The word *kosher* means "proper, correct"; it is applied to religious objects or religious behavior. For example, a Torah Scroll that meets all the ritual requirements is referred to as *"kosher"*; one that does not is spoken of as "not *kosher*." The term, however, is most often used in connection with the dietary laws.

There are those who believe the purpose of the dietary laws to be a safeguard of good health. However, as Rabbi Samuel Dresner has pointed out, the clear purpose and goal of these laws is not health, but *holiness*. Passages in Exodus, Leviticus, and Deuteronomy which present the biblical basis of these laws always include statements that these laws are to help us to become holy, as God Himself is holy. Whatever hygienic advantages may have accrued to Jews from observing *kashrut,* they are secondary.

In chapter eleven of the Book of Leviticus, forty-four verses of instruction about dietary laws are followed by the statement: "I am the Lord your God; sanctify yourselves therefore and be holy, for I am holy." Permitted and prohibited foods help to shape a way of life that reflects sanctity. It is part of a total way of life that trains us to control our animal instincts. It is a dietary discipline undertaken not in order to lose weight, not in order to become more attractive, not even to promote health, but to help infuse all of life with a sense of holiness.

Although the teachers of Judaism never went so far as to insist on vegetarianism, the Torah implies that it was an ideal. In the Garden of Eden, Adam and Eve ate no meat. After the Flood, the permission granted Noah to eat meat seems to be a concession to human weakness. Animals are also creatures of God. If we take their lives for the sake of our own sustenance, we are obliged to do so in a restricted way, one in which the animal experiences a minimum of pain. Jewish tradition teaches reverence for all life in many ways; one of these ways is by trying to hallow the act of eating and the preparations which it entails.

People who accept the Torah as divine need no rationale for *kashrut,* a discipline commanded by God. Those who consider the Torah to be holy but not necessarily literally revealed accept *kashrut* as a part of religion which adds meaning to their lives.

The meat of certain animals may not be eaten, as stated in the Torah. Those permitted must have cloven hooves and chew the cud; this eliminates the flesh of pigs and rabbits, for example. The life of the animal is taken only in the manner prescribed by Jewish law. The slaughterer is called a *shoḥet.* The *shoḥet* must be knowledgeable as well as pious. The sharp knife he uses must be tested periodically for nicks and dullness. He must know enough about anatomy to insure a minimum of pain to the animal, as well as to detect the slightest malfunctioning of an organ, because the flesh of an animal which was diseased or had certain types of blemishes may not be eaten. If there is any question, a rabbinic authority must be consulted to decide whether or not the meat may be used. Forbidden food is designated *taref,* often pronounced *treif.* (The word literally means "to tear to pieces," and originally applied to forbidding the flesh of animals which had died as the result of an attack.)

Eating blood is forbidden, for "blood is life," as the Torah teaches, and life is sacred. Meat is rid of blood by soaking it in cold water for half an hour in a utensil used only for this purpose. It then is sprinkled liberally with salt and drained on an inclined, perforated board for an hour. After it is rinsed with cold running water, it is free of blood. This may be done at home, though generally today it is done at the butcher shop. Liver or steaks that are to be broiled need not be salted, because they become free of blood through broiling. They need only be rinsed with cold water and placed over or under an open fire.

Fowl must also be slaughtered by a *shoḥet.* Fish do not have to be slaughtered, of course, but only fish with scales and fins are kosher. Other seafood, such as eels and shellfish, are *taref* and forbidden.

*Kashrut* requires the separation of meat from milk. The basis for this is also biblical. Meat and milk, and their products, may not be cooked or eaten together. They may not be prepared or even eaten at separate times using the same utensils and plates. All dishes, utensils, serving dishes, sponges, and dish towels used for meat must be totally different and separate from those used for milk. Meat and meat derivatives are referred to by the Yiddish word *fleishig*. Milk and milk products are referred to as *milchig*. In *kosher* homes, different colors or different markings help to differentiate the two sets, often red for *fleishig* and blue for *milchig*.

Some foods are neither *fleishig* nor *milchig*. They are called *paraveh*. Fruit, vegetables, grains, fish, and eggs are *paraveh*. They may be eaten with either *milchig* or *fleishig* foods.

Although it is permissable to use one set of glass dishes for both *milchig* and *fleishig* (because they can be thoroughly cleaned and are not porous), the practice is not encouraged since it does away with the idea of separation which is an important aspect of *kashrut*.

Keeping a *kosher* home appears complicated to the uninitiated, but it is not significantly more difficult than non-*kosher* housekeeping. You soon become accustomed to reading labels in the supermarket to make sure that packaged goods which appear to be *paraveh* really are, to notice which products have milk or milk derivatives in them, to make sure that baked goods were not cooked with lard or beef suet. *Kosher* meat is somewhat more expensive because more people are involved in producing it than is the case for other meat. Those who keep *kosher* obviously feel the observance to be so important that it is worth the expense. Many people have become vegetarians because they disagree with slaughtering animals for food, and because it is easier to keep *kosher* when there is no meat in the house.

Eating out in non-*kosher* restaurants or in the homes of people who do not keep *kosher* causes some difficulties. Orthodox Jews will not eat anything from plates in homes or restaurants which serve non-*kosher* food. Some Conservative Jews also adopt this standard. Others, in order to participate more fully in the general community, adopt a more lenient legal position. Thus, for example, they will eat nonmeat products in most restaurants or homes. They request salads, cheese, pasta, fruit, broiled fish, and vegetarian dishes. Reform Jews do not regard the dietary laws as binding, though some refrain from eating those foods specifically prohibited in Leviticus.

Before and after eating, observant Jews remind themselves of God's gifts as they express gratitude with various appropriate blessings. These *berakhot* also remind us not to take food for granted. For example, this *berakhah* is recited before eating bread (by itself or at the start of a meal):

> *Barukh atah Adonai Eloheinu melekh ha-olam hamotzi leḥem min ha-aretz.*
>
> Praised are You, Lord our God, King of the Universe who brings forth bread from the earth.

This *berakhah* is recited before one drinks wine (or grape juice):

> *Barukh atah Adonai Eloheinu melekh ha-olam borei pri ha-gafen.*
>
> Praised are You, Lord our God, King of the Universe who creates the fruit of the vine.

The prayerbook contains many more texts of *berakhot* for various occasions, such as seeing the first buds in spring, hearing thunder, smelling spices, and upon receiving good, or bad, news.

After meals, *birkat hamazon* is recited. The first *berakhah* of these blessings also furnishes another example of the universal dimension of Jewish tradition:

> Praised are You, Lord our God, King of the universe who sustains the whole world with kindness and with compassion. He provides food for every creature, for His love endures forever. His great goodness has never failed us, His great glory assures us

nourishment. All life is His creation and He is good to all, providing every creature with food and sustenance. Praised are You, Lord who sustains all life.

SHABBAT

Shabbat (pronounced *shabbos* in Ashkenazic Hebrew and in Yiddish) is the climax of the week. It is the day associated with peace, as reflected in the greeting *Shabbat Shalom* (*Shalom* means peace; another greeting is "Good *Shabbos*"). Jewish tradition considers Shabbat to be a foretaste of Paradise. Poets speak of this day as a bride and as a queen. One of the Ten Commandments refers to it as a reminder of both Creation and the Exodus from Egypt. The centrality of Shabbat is reflected in the Hebrew names for the days of the week, which are all related to Shabbat. Sunday, for example, is "the first day," Monday is "the second day," and so forth.

Many descriptions of Shabbat have attempted to capture its purpose and mood. Rachel Rabinowicz, in her comments to the Passover *Haggadah,* has written that "Shabbat, one of God's greatest gifts to Israel, is one of Israel's greatest gifts to humanity. Shabbat spans the ages, from the beginning of time to the End of Days. In its observance we become partners in creation, and in its transcendent tranquility we glimpse the world to come."

Perhaps the most eloquent and authentic words about Shabbat have been written in modern times by Dr. Abraham Joshua Heschel in *The Sabbath* and in *God in Search of Man.*

The seventh day is the armistice in man's cruel struggle for existence, a truce in all conflicts, personal and social . . . a day on which handling money is considered a desecration, on which man avows his independence of that which is the world's chief idol. The seventh day is the exodus from tension, the installation of man as a sovereign in the world of time.

What is the Sabbath? A reminder of every man's royalty; an abolition of the distinction of master and slave, rich and poor, success and failure. To celebrate the Sabbath is to experience one's ultimate independence of civilization and society, of achievement and anxiety. The Sabbath is an embodiment of the belief that all men are equal and that equality of men means the nobility of men. The greatest sin of man is to forget that he is a prince.

The Sabbath is an assurance that the spirit is greater than the universe, that beyond the good is the holy. The universe was created in six days, but the climax of creation was the seventh day. Things that came into being in the six days are good, but the seventh day is holy. The Sabbath is holiness in time.

What is the Sabbath? The presence of eternity, a moment of majesty, the radiance of joy. The soul is enhanced, time is a delight, and inwardness a supreme reward. Indignation is felt to be a desecration of the day, and strife the suicide of one's additional soul. Man does not stand alone, he lives in the presence of the day.

The Sabbath is known as a day of rest. The concept of rest on Shabbat often has been misunderstood. As Rabbi Louis Jacobs has written, "The Sabbath ideal of rest is not purely passive, a mere stoppage of labor. A special atmosphere of difference from other days is cultivated by refraining from weekday pursuits as well as by the wearing of special Sabbath clothes, by the lighted candles, the best tablecloth, the cup of wine over which God is hailed as Creator . . ."

Finally, another quote from Dr. Heschel. "Six days a week we live under the tyranny of things of space; on the Sabbath we try to become attuned to *holiness in time*. It is a day on which we are called upon to share what is eternal in time, to turn from the results of creation to the mystery of creation; from the world of creation to the creation of the world."

The Sabbath begins on Friday night before dusk. It is introduced at home by lighting candles, accompanied by a *berakhah*. Traditionally, women light the candles. Children sometimes join in saying the *berakhah*. In the absence of a woman, a man should light the Sabbath and Festival candles. Today some couples take turns lighting them. Unmarried people in their own homes should also light candles. Many people, after reciting the Hebrew *berakhah,* add their own personal silent prayer or meditation.

Before the *Shabbat* meal, *kiddush* is chanted at the table. Traditionally, men recite *kiddush,* but in some households today women share this obligation. *Kiddush,* which means sanctification, expresses gratitude to God for the gift of Shabbat. It is chanted over a cup of wine, symbol of joy. After *kiddush,* everyone drinks some wine.

The table is set with a fresh cloth and the best dishes and wine cups in honor of Shabbat. Fresh flowers often adorn the home as well. In a place of honor on the table are two covered loaves of *ḥallah.* *Ḥallah* is braided egg bread, traditionally associated with the Sabbath. The two loaves recall the double portion of manna that God gave the Israelites in the wilderness before Shabbat (so that they would not have to gather manna on Shabbat itself). They also recall the two loaves of bread placed on the altar in the ancient Temple.

Before the *berakhah* for the bread *(hamotzi)* is recited, there is a ritual washing of the hands. Water is poured over each hand from a pitcher or cup and a *berakhah* is recited. Then *hamotzi* is recited over the *ḥallah,* and pieces are distributed to all. Some people sprinkle salt on the *ḥallah* as a reminder of the Temple ritual during which salt was sprinkled on some of the offerings. There is also a tradition that this gesture recalls the atoning power of the Temple ritual at the altar. In some homes, just before *kiddush,* the father blesses his children with the words of the priestly blessing (Numbers 6:22−24):

> May the Lord bless you and keep you.
> May the Lord show you favor and be gracious to you.
> May the lord show you kindness and grant you peace.

He then adds, for boys: "May the Lord make you as Ephraim and Manasseh." For girls he adds: "May the Lord make you as Sarah, Rebecca, Rachel, and Leah." In some homes, both parents formally bless the children.

There is no required menu, but certain dishes have come to be associated with the warmth and uniqueness of Shabbat dining: *gefilte* fish, chicken soup, and roast chicken. Whatever the food may be, Shabbat is an occasion for a royal banquet at which we are enriched by special food and a special spirit.

After services on Saturday morning, people return home to another Shabbat meal. This meal, too, is begun with *kiddush* over a cup of wine and with *hamotzi* over two *ḥallot* (plural of *ḥallah*). Many families sing Sabbath songs *(zemirot)* before chanting the blessings after meals on Friday night and on Saturday. The afternoon is spent quietly, featuring naps, leisurely walks, companionship of family and friends, and study. Some congregations hold classes in the late afternoon. Mourning is not permitted on Shabbat. Neither is fasting (unless *Yom Kippur* happens to be on Saturday; it is the only day whose ritual takes precedence over that of Shabbat).

Since eating is considered essential to the enjoyment of the Sabbath, three full meals are to be eaten. The first is on Friday evening, the second is at midday on Saturday, and the third is to be eaten before dark. This does not have to be an elaborate meal, but it should include bread so that *hamotzi* may be recited before the meal and *birkat hamazon* after the meal. This meal is known by its Hebrew name: *seudah shlishit* (literally, "third meal"). In some synagogues, *seudah shlishit* is served to those who gather for the late afternoon and evening services.

The Sabbath concludes each week about one hour after the time of candlelighting on Sabbath Eve (candlelighting is about twenty minutes before sunset, though it may be done earlier). Just as the Sabbath was ushered in with a religious ceremony, it is escorted out with one. This ceremony is called *havdalah* (literally "distinction"). It affirms the distinction between the holy and the secular, between the Sabbath and the weekday. At *havdalah* a braided candle is lit and held. The person chanting the *berakhot* and other passages holds a cup of wine. A container of spices *(besamim)* is passed around for all to sniff; spices symbolically restore vitality to us, as we are each diminished by the departure of Shabbat.

One of the prominent features of Shabbat and other holy days is the prohibition of work. Working is not defined solely as expenditure of energy or earning a livelihood. It is a religious-legal concept worked out by the rabbis in the postbiblical era. It includes acts which most people do not ordinarily think of as labor—for example, it is prohibited to write, sew, cut, or use money. Carrying from public space to private or *vice versa* is defined as "work" on Shabbat. Since no fire may be kindled, cooking, baking, and smoking are not permitted on the Sabbath. Orthodox authorities extend the prohibition of kindling a fire to electricity. Most Conservative authorities do not regard electricity as fire and therefore permit its use. Reform authorities regard all these prohibitions as no longer binding. There is a prohibition against riding on the Sabbath and the holy days. Because people today often live great distances from the synagogue, the Rabbinical Assembly Committee on Jewish Law and Standards has ruled that it is permitted to ride to the synagogue and back home if one would not otherwise be able to participate in public worship. This permission to ride is not extended to riding for other purposes.

The fact that so many acts are forbidden does not make the Sabbath or holy days austere or gloomy. To the contrary, they are days of joy and of great spiritual delight, distinct from ordinary days. People who observe them through prayer, study, and companionship are physically and spiritually renewed.

Dr. Abraham Joshua Heschel helped us to appreciate the Sabbath more deeply when he wrote in *The Sabbath:*

> The art of keeping the seventh day is the art of painting on the canvas of time the mysterious grandeur of the climax of creation:

as He sanctified the seventh day, so shall we. The love of the
Sabbath is the love of man for what he and God have in common. Our keeping the Sabbath day is a paraphrase of His sanctification of the seventh day.

STUDY

Study is a basic religious obligation in Jewish tradition. People
who seek to shape committed religious lives establish a fixed period of study each week. The Bible, especially the Torah, and the
Talmud are their obvious choices, but they study other texts as
well.

Religious fulfillment requires more than the performance of
ritual law; it must include dedication to study, to Torah. The
rabbis long ago asserted that ignorant people cannot be truly
pious. Judaism cannot survive without learning. A well-known
Talmudic story dramatically illustrates this conviction.

The great Rabbi Akiba lived in the second century, when the
Empire of Rome was determined to put an end to the Jewish
faith which it considered heretical. Realizing that physical force
had failed to achieve the goal, the emperor issued a decree forbidding Jews to practice ritual circumcision, to observe Shabbat,
or to teach Torah. Jews who wanted to survive as Jews had no
choice but to defy such decrees. Accordingly, the sages continued to meet with their disciples to pursue the path of Torah. The
revered Rabbi Akiba refused to teach surreptitiously. He met his
students openly. One of his friends, aware of the consequences
of this act, urged him to desist. Rabbi Akiba responded with this
fable:

"A fox on a river bank noticed the frantic movement of fish
in the water. He asked them why they were so agitated, and was
told that fishermen had come to the river intent upon catching
fish. Thereupon the fox invited the fish to leave the water to join
him on dry land where they would be safe. The fish replied to the
fox, 'And they call you the wisest of creatures? If we cannot sur-

vive in water, which is our natural habitat, we surely cannot survive *outside* it!' "

"Thus it is with us," concluded Rabbi Akiba. "If we cannot survive with Torah, which is 'our life and the length of our days,' we surely cannot survive without it." And he continued to teach until he was arrested, imprisoned, and put to a martyr's death.

Throughout the centuries, Jews have always insisted that learning is an obligation. Jewish life has been guided by the rabbinic maxim "If you possess knowledge, what can you lack? If you lack knowledge, what can you possess?" Mothers sang lullabies to infants in cradles praising Torah as the most valuable of all acquisitions. Moses, the greatest figure of Jewish history, is extolled as liberator and lawgiver, but he is known primarily as *Moshe Rabbeinu,* Moses our teacher. Classically, the heroes of the Jewish people have been students of Torah. In the European community, when a man undertook to find a husband for his daughter, he did not look for someone who could provide her with luxuries but someone who gave promise of becoming a great scholar. The rich man who was ignorant was not as honored or respected as the impoverished man whose life was dedicated to study.

In the contemporary world, this standard usually is given mere lip service if noted at all. Jews have absorbed the values of the society in which they live. Jewish scholarship no longer ranks as the most precious possession. The traditional passion for learning has often been transferred to secular studies, while Jewish learning has been neglected. The resulting unfamiliarity with and alienation from the sources have weakened the quality of Jewish life. Many people who feel strongly identified with the Jewish people are basically ignorant about Judaism. This situation threatens the continuation of a meaningful way of religious life and endangers commitment to Jewish principles. Many are now working hard to revive the traditional emphasis on Jewish education and to develop creative approaches so that Jews as a community will continue to be what Muhammad once called us: "The People of the Book."

## Suggested Readings for Further Study

Donin, Haim Halevy, *To Be a Jew* (New York: Basic Books, 1972)

Dresner, Samuel, and Siegel, Seymour; and Pollack, David, *The Jewish Dietary Laws* (New York: The Rabbinical Assembly and the United Synagogue Commission on Jewish Education, 1982)

Dresner, Samuel, *The Sabbath* (New York: Burning Bush Press, 1970)

Heschel, Abraham Joshua, *The Sabbath* (New York: Farrar, Straus and Young, 1951)

Levi, Shonie, and Kaplan, Sylvia, *Guide for the Jewish Homemaker* (New York: Schocken Books, 1965)

ADDITIONAL SUGGESTIONS

Klein, Isaac, *A Guide to Jewish Religious Practice* (New York: The Jewish Theological Seminary, 1979)

Lebeau, James M., *The Jewish Dietary Laws: Sanctify Life* (New York: United Synagogue of America)

Millgram, Abraham, *The Sabbath: A Day of Delight* (Philadelphia: The Jewish Publication Society, 1944)

Siegel, Richard, and Strassfeld, Michael and Sharon, *The Jewish Catalogue* (Philadelphia: The Jewish Publication Society, 1973)

Trepp, Leo, *The Complete Book of Jewish Observance* (New York: Behrman House, Summit Books, 1980)

# CHAPTER 7

# The Jewish Life Cycle

*A*LL significant events in the life of a Jew are accompanied by prayers and ceremonies. These special prayers and ceremonies help us to become aware of the holiness of these occasions.

### Birth

The most basic ceremony for infant Jewish males has become such a common contemporary practice that many have forgotten its original purpose. Circumcision is a religious rite for Jews. Although many others have adopted it for hygienic reasons, it is not a health measure for Jewish tradition.

The circumcision ceremony is known in Hebrew as a *brit,* which means covenant. Technically, it is called *brit milah,* "covenant of circumcision." Most people know it as a *bris.* Through this ritual act each infant boy becomes linked to the covenant that God made with the Jewish people.

As a religious ceremony, the *brit* must be carried out by a

Jew trained in religious law, who performs the act as the conscious fulfillment of a religious commandment *(mitzvah)*. This person, called a *mohel,* must be certified by medical authorites as well.

Circumcision must take place on the eighth day after birth. We read in the Book of Genesis that Isaac was circumcised on the eighth day. So must it be with all the children of Abraham. In the event of illness or other disability, the child is circumcised when the physician declares him to be physically ready. If the baby is born without a foreskin or for some reason has been circumcised prior to the eighth day, the ritual of circumcision is completed by drawing a drop of blood from the tip of the penis. This ceremony (called *hatafat dam brit*) is also required for an adult male convert who was circumcised prior to his conversion.

At the *brit milah* ceremony, certain individuals are honored. Although the English term "godparents" is sometimes used for these people, they are not godparents in the Christian sense of the term. At the *brit milah,* three individuals are simply given honors, and in the English-speaking world they are designated as "godparents." The Yiddish word for "godmother" is *kvaterin*; she brings the infant forward and hands him to the *kvater* (the Yiddish word for "godfather"). The *kvater* places the infant on the knees of the *sandek,* who is already seated. Often the *sandek* holds the infant while the *mohel* performs the circumcision. The *sandek* could be the child's grandfather or some other attendee whom the family wishes to honor.

The *mohel* recites a *berakhah*. The father recites another *berakhah* after the circumcision is completed. Then the boy is named. There are no laws regarding names. Parents often spend many hours in choosing a name for their child. The general practice is to give the child an English name that has some connection with the Hebrew name declared at the ceremony. It can be an Anglicized version of the Hebrew (for example, Joseph for *Yosef,* or Miriam for *Miryam*); it can be an English name that has the same meaning as the Hebrew or Yiddish name (for example:

Wolf for *Zev,* or Joy for *Frayda*); it can even be a name that has the same first initial as the Hebrew name. The custom among Ashkenazim (Jews of Central or Eastern European background) is to name the child for a deceased relative or friend. The Sefardim name their children for living relatives. Many people coin new Hebrew names or choose names from the Bible or from rabbinic literature.

The birth of a daughter is marked in another fashion, since there is no traditional ceremony for a girl parallel to a *brit.* She is named soon after her birth in the synagogue at a service when the Torah is read. (Some people today, not satisfied with this practice, have been developing additional ceremonies to celebrate the birth of a daughter.) The child need not be present at the naming ceremony in the synagogue. If the mother is well enough to attend services, she obviously is welcome. The father is honored by being called to the Torah. In congregations where women are given *aliyot,* the mother may be similarly honored. A prayer is recited wishing parents and child a long and healthy life marked by good deeds and fulfillment.

Another ritual is required when a woman's firstborn child is a boy. The ceremony is called *pidyon haben* (literally, Redemption of the Son). The practice goes back to ancient Temple times. The Torah states that all firstborn males are to be consecrated to God.

> In early biblical times, the first-born son in every Israelite family was vested with special responsibilities. From the day of his birth he was consecrated to the vocation of assisting the priests in the conduct of worship.
>
> Later, when a Tabernacle was built in the wilderness, this vocation of the firstborn was transferred to the Levites, a priestly tribe. The Torah then decreed that every father release his firstborn son from the duties incumbent upon all firstborn sons by redeeming him from a *Kohen.* The ancient obligations of the firstborn son thus continue to be recalled.

Since the Priests and Levites were part of the Temple establishment, their children did not need to be "redeemed." Therefore, no *pidyon haben* is held if either parent is the child of a *kohen* or of a *levi*. Some contemporaries are developing a parallel ceremony for a firstborn daughter, calling it *pidyon habat*.

### Bar Mitzvah and Bat Mitzvah

The new teenager, not quite an adult and no longer a child, is beginning to mature intellectually as well as physically. The terms *Bar Mitzvah* and *Bat Mitzvah* refer to the boy and girl who are obligated to fulfill religious duties *(mitzvot)* now that they have attained their religious majority. Boys at age 13 and girls at age 12 are considered old enough to assume these responsibilities. A *Bar Mitzvah* is included as one of the adults who constitute a *minyan* (quorum of ten) which is necessary in order to hold a public worship service. A *Bat Mitzvah* also counts for a *minyan* in congregations that accept women in this capacity. A *Bar* and *Bat Mitzvah* are obliged to fast on *Yom Kippur* and to observe the other *mitzvot*.

Attaining the status of *Bar Mitzvah* or *Bat Mitzvah* is an important milestone in a person's life. It is marked at a worship service. One is officially recognized as *Bar* or *Bat Mitzvah* by being called to the Torah. (In Orthodox and some Conservative congregations where women do not receive *aliyot,* the *bat mitzvah* ceremony may take place during a service where the Torah is not read, or after a service at which the Torah is read. Sometimes the young girl chants or reads passages from other parts of the Bible. She may also present a brief lesson which she has prepared.) The ceremony usually takes place on Shabbat mornings, but it may be held at any service when the Torah is read. In most congregations, the *Bar* or *Bat Mitzvah* is honored by being called to recite the blessings for the *maftir* portion, and then to chant the *haftarah*. They thus show that they are able to participate in services as a full member of the congregation. Sometimes they also lead in chanting parts of the prayer service, or read part or all of the Torah portion.

It must be remembered that this is not a private birthday party but a ceremony signifying one's willingness and ability to become a responsible member of the Jewish community. The ceremony usually takes place close to the celebrant's thirteenth birthday (twelfth, for girls), but it may take place at any time afterward. Many adults who never formally became a *Bat* or *Bar Mitzvah* find it very meaningful to have an official ceremony after they have learned to read the Torah or to chant the *haftarah*.

## Marriage

The Hebrew word for marriage is *kiddushin,* which means holiness. That word reflects the Jewish view of marriage. During the wedding ceremony, God is praised for enabling a man and a woman to find fulfillment through marriage. As the Book of Genesis declares, "It is not good for man to dwell alone."

The wedding ceremony is held under a canopy called a *ḥuppah,* which symbolizes the home which the couple is about to establish. According to Jewish law, two witnesses who are not blood relatives of the bride or groom must formally witness the ceremony and sign the marriage contract *(ketubah)*.

The ceremony consists of two parts. The first is called *erusin* (betrothal). In ancient times, a man and a woman were legally bound to one another at betrothal. After that ceremony, they returned to their parental homes to prepare for the wedding, which could take place several months later. In later years, however, the betrothal and the wedding ceremonies were combined into one ceremony under the *ḥuppah*. *Erusin* consists of two blessings praising God and thanking Him for the institution of marriage.

The groom places a ring on the bride's right forefinger (the most prominent finger, on which brides wore their wedding ring in ancient times. Later the ring is shifted to the usual finger). As he does so, he says in Hebrew (and sometimes in English as well):

"Behold you are consecrated to me with this ring according to the law of Moses and the people Israel." Many contemporary brides place a ring on the groom's finger and recite another passage, chosen in consultation with the rabbi, to reflect a similar sense of consecration.

The ring ceremony is followed by the reading of the marriage contract *(ketubah)*. Traditionally, the *ketubah* states the basic obligations undertaken by the husband for his wife. Today many couples request that the *ketubah* be accompanied by statements describing mutual obligations and responsibilities. The rabbi may read all or part of the *ketubah* aloud.

The service continues with blessings called *birkhot nesuin* (the last word means "wedding"). Seven blessings *(sheva berakhot)* are chanted, praising God for the creation of man and woman, that together they might perpetuate life. This is a translation of the final two *berakhot*:

> Grant perfect joy to these loving companions, as You did to the first man and woman in the Garden of Eden. Praised are You, Lord who grants the joy of bride and groom.

> Praised are You, Lord our God, King of the universe who created joy and gladness, bride and groom, mirth, song, delight and rejoicing, love and harmony, peace and companionship. O Lord our God, may there ever be heard in the cities of Judah and in the streets of Jerusalem voices of joy and gladness, voices of bride and groom, the jubilant voices of those joined in marriage beneath the bridal canopy, the voices of young people feasting and singing. Praised are You, Lord who causes the groom to rejoice with his bride.

At the conclusion of the service the groom steps on a glass and breaks it. (Sometimes a light bulb or other fragile glass object is used.) Even at the moment of their greatest joy, the newly married couple thus remember that they are part of the Jewish people, not isolated individuals. The breaking of the glass recalls the destruction of the ancient Temple in Jerusalem.

It is customary for a rabbi to speak to the bride and groom at some point during this ceremony. There is no uniform practice in this matter.

## *Divorce*

For those marriages which do not work out, divorce is accepted in Judaism; the grounds for it include adultery and incompatibility. Couples who are mismatched need not remain bound to each other, although rabbis encourage them to seek counseling with the goal of working out their problems together. Divorce may be the only solution for frustrated lives and an unhappy home.

When a husband and wife reach a parting of the ways, they must obtain a religious divorce. Just as the marriage begins with a religious document, so must it end. If the couple lives in a country that requires a civil divorce, they obtain that before turning to a rabbi. The early rabbis found the precedent for divorce in Deuteronomy (24:1): "He writes her a bill of divorcement, hands it to her, and sends her away from his house." They decided that Jewish religious procedure should require the husband to initiate the divorce proceedings. The rabbi, two witnesses, and the husband (or his agent) must be present as the divorce document—called *get*—is begun and completed. The *get* must be written by a scribe for the specific man and woman involved; it cannot be a printed form with blanks for names to be inserted. After the document is signed and witnessed, it must be put into the hands of the wife or her agent.

The Reform movement has waived the requirement for a *get* and accepts a civil divorce as sufficient. The Orthodox and Conservative movements follow the traditional ruling that a husband and wife remain legally bound to one another unless they have a Jewish divorce. They cannot remarry in the Jewish tradition without having obtained a *get*.

In the days when Jews lived in self-contained communities,

a clearly unfit husband could be forced to give his wife a *get*. Social pressure was strong enough to ensure compliance with a rabbinic decision. In an open society, however, it is difficult to force a recalcitrant husband to comply. In some instances, men have used the Jewish divorce as a means of extortion, refusing to give the *get* until a substantial sum has been paid. The Orthodox rabbinate has been looking for a way in Jewish law to overcome this problem. The Conservative rabbinate has solved the problem by inserting in the *ketubah* a passage stating that in the event of marital difficulties, the couple agrees to abide by the decision of a court convened by the Rabbinical Assembly and the Jewish Theological Seminary. Since this is signed and witnessed, it is a legal document which could be enforced in a civil court. There are those who plead with the contemporary rabbinate to give a woman the right to divorce her husband just as the tradition gives a man the right to divorce his wife. However, those responsible for interpreting Jewish law have thus far not found a way to do so.

## Death and Mourning

Jewish tradition helps mourners to confront death with a sense of reality and dignity. The sages who drew up the laws of mourning recognized that mourners need a time when they can grieve unrestrainedly. Before the burial, mourners need time to be alone with their grief, as well as to focus on making arrangements for the funeral and burial. Jewish tradition does not provide for or encourage anything similar to a wake. It is not considered helpful or proper for mourners to be at a funeral home or anywhere else the evening before a burial for the purpose of receiving visitors. Visits to comfort mourners should be made only after the funeral, when such visits are the fulfillment of a religious obligation.

The funeral is held as soon as possible after death. Unless a delay is necessary to give relatives time to travel great distances, the funeral should be held within 24 hours of the death (unless Shabbat begins during that period). The body is ritually washed and watched—it is never left alone—before the funeral. Sometimes the washing and watching are arranged for by the funeral home, sometimes by members of a congregational or community burial society *(ḥevrah kadishah)* who regard caring for the dead as an extremely important *mitzvah*. The body is dressed in a white linen shroud and placed in a plain wooden coffin. Rituals involving the funeral and burial are similar for all Jews regardless of social or economic status.

It is traditional at Jewish funerals not to adorn the coffin with flowers. It is appropriate to honor the dead by contributing to a cause which was meaningful to him or her and which will help the living.

Jewish law forbids cremation. The rabbis who formulated the law took the verse "for you are dust and unto dust shall you return" (Genesis 3:19) literally as a natural process.

Funerals in the past were conducted at home or at the cemetery. In North America today, most funerals take place in funeral parlors. Funerals for rabbis, scholars, or other prominent members of the congregation may be held in a synagogue.

There is no fixed procedure for the funeral service. The rabbi, or other leader, recites various psalms and other appropriate passages from biblical and rabbinic sources. In the past, eulogies were delivered only for the learned; today they are a part of most funerals. The funeral concludes with a prayer *(el malei raḥamim)* that God grant the departed complete peace in His sheltering Presence, that the soul of the departed be bound up in the bond of life, and that the departed rest in peace.

According to Jewish law, one is obliged to mourn for a father, mother, son, daughter, brother, sister, husband, or wife. Others who are not *obliged* to mourn may also participate in the mourning rituals. At the funeral, mourners tear their garments as a sign of sorrow. This is called *keriah* (tearing). Since this may ruin expensive garments, some people first remove the stitches in a seam. Others pin a black ribbon to their clothing, after which the ribbon is cut to symbolize their grief.

At the cemetery, psalms and other passages as well as a prayer may be read at graveside. The mourners recite the Mourner's *Kaddish* for the first time. In some communities, relatives and friends find it meaningful to participate in placing dirt into the grave. It is appropriate that they, rather than strangers, at least initiate this final step of burial.

The mourners return home to begin observing a seven-day period of mourning known as *shivah* (which means seven). They do not leave the house during this week, except to attend synagogue services on Shabbat, when public mourning is suspended. It is traditional for friends to prepare the first meal after the funeral and to bring food for the mourners and their visitors during the rest of the week when members of the community and other friends come to express their sympathy. Out of respect for the feelings of the mourners, it is customary not to initiate conversations with them but rather to wait until the mourners feel like talking. The most appropriate topic of conversation is to recall the life of the person who died. Visitors are also needed when morning, afternoon, and evening services are held, to constitute a *minyan* which enables the mourners to recite the Mourner's *Kaddish* in the home. If a *minyan* cannot be provided at home, the mourners attend services at a synagogue, after which they return home.

In many homes, all mirrors are covered during the *shivah* period. Although probably rooted in superstition, this practice today is a statement that vanity and self-pity are not appropriate at a time of such grief. Mourners sit on low stools rather than on regular chairs. They do not wear leather shoes, another sign of mourning. Men do not shave during the week of *shivah* (some do not shave for thirty days, and some do not shave for a year).

After *shivah*, mourners enter a stage of transition from deep bereavement to resuming their normal routine. This stage ends on the morning of the thirtieth day after the funeral, and it is called *shloshim* (meaning thirty). During *shloshim* people may go back to work. However, they do not attend parties, plays, movies, or concerts and generally do not participate in joyous occasions, although they may fulfill the mitzvah of attending certain religious ceremonies, such as a wedding ceremony. Some people who have lost a parent observe these restrictions for one year.

After *shloshim,* mourners attend services every morning and evening for an additional ten months, at which they recite the Mourner's *Kaddish.* Children continue to recite *Kaddish* every year on the *yahrzeit* (anniversary of the death) and at *yizkor* (memorial) services on *Yom Kippur,* and on the three Pilgrimage Festivals, (Passover, *Shavuot,* and *Sukkot*). A memorial candle which burns for twenty-four hours is lit on the *yahrzeit* and at *Yom Kippur.*

What happens after death is a mystery that human beings can never fathom. There is no single definitive Jewish teaching about life after death. Jews have always held a variety of views. Many have believed that the dead will be resurrected, but there always have been those who do not take this teaching literally. For some additional thoughts on this subject, please consult Chapter 2, under "Teachings on the Afterlife." Whatever their particular view, most religious Jews believe that physical death is not the final end of human life.

"Is death nothing but an obliteration, an absolute negation?" The question was posed by Dr. Abraham Joshua Heschel, who then stated that our view of death "is affected by our understanding of life. If life is sensed as a surprise, as a gift, defying explanation, then death ceases to be a radical, absolute negation of what life stands for. For both life and death are aspects of a greater mystery, the mystery of being, the mystery of creation. . . . The meaning of death is in return, regardless of whether it results in a continuation of individual consciousness or in merging into a greater whole. We are what we are by what we come from. We achieve what we do by what we hope for. Our ultimate hope has no specific content. Our hope is God. We trust that He will not desert those who trust in Him."

## *Suggested Readings for Further Study*

Greenberg, Blu, *How to Run a Traditional Jewish Household* (New York: Simon and Schuster, 1983)

Rosenberg, Devorah, *The Three Pillars* (New York: The Women's League for Conservative Judaism, 1984)

ADDITIONAL SUGGESTIONS

Goodman, Philip and Hanna, editors, *The Jewish Marriage Anthology* (Philadelphia: The Jewish Publication Society, 1968)

Kushner, Harold, *When Bad Things Happen to Good People* (New York: Schocken Books, 1981)

Lamm, Maurice, *The Jewish Way in Death and Mourning* (New York: Jonathan David Publishers, 1969)

———, *The Jewish Way in Love and Marriage* (New York: Harper and Row, 1980)

Schneid, Hayyim, *Marriage* (Philadelphia: The Jewish Publication Society, 1973)

# CHAPTER 8

# History: Ancient and Medieval

*T*HE Jews are an ancient people with a keen sense of history. History is not only a matter of the past for Jews. It continues to function in every generation. Heroes and events of the past become almost contemporary; spiritual and moral insights from ancient times guide the conduct and inform the decisions of all generations. Jews of any one period do not think and live precisely as their ancestors did, but their thoughts and lives are very much rooted in those who preceded them. Thus, every Jewish community in each period of history has been an organic development of that which went before.

Since Jewish thought, practice, and faith regard past and present as parts of a continuous whole, it is imperative to gain familiarity with Jewish history. This outline of Jewish history should serve only as the beginning of further study.

## The Torah

The history of the Jews begins with the Torah. In one sense, it is narrative history with God as the prime force. The Torah is also a history of the development of Jewish ideas. It relates a history that itself has shaped events.

Significantly, the Torah begins not with an account of the origins of the Jewish people but with the creation of the universe. Jews regard God not as their exclusive sovereign but as Master of the entire world and Lord of all. Since the Torah is a religious document rather than a book of science, what is significant about Genesis is the eternal message of Creation. The description there is not to be taken literally. Genesis asserts that the universe is not an accident, not the result of purposeless chance or divine caprice. It was created by God who so willed it and who is involved in its history.

God created human beings as well, and endowed them with divine potential. We have the ability to transcend our animal nature because we possess spiritual qualities. The Torah insists that human life is not determined by blind fate.

This was a radical assertion in the ancient world. All other people firmly believed that human beings had no control over their destiny. The very essence of paganism was its premise that the universe is controlled by fate. The gods themselves were subject to it, not free to act as they wished. The Torah, however, teaches that God endowed men and women with the ability to choose between good and evil, making them responsible for the consequences of their choices.

Abraham believed paganism's premise to be false. He worshiped one all-powerful Lord of the Universe, a just and righteous God. In order to be true to his vision and to train others to share it, Abraham left his home in highly civilized Mesopotamia and went to a new land. Canaan was the land of destiny for him and for his descendants. Abraham's new religion was a family matter at first. He passed it on to his son Isaac who transmitted it to his son Jacob (who later was given the name of Israel). The children of the third patriarch, confronted by a severe famine in Canaan, moved to Egypt temporarily but became trapped by a change of regimes. A new nativist dynasty came to power and enslaved foreigners. The children of Israel endured a long, harsh bondage, but throughout they retained their sense of kinship and remembered their ancestors' teachings.

Moses, the man who led the slaves out of Egypt, was one of the most remarkable spiritual geniuses of all time. Under his leadership, the Israelites were transformed from a mass of terrified slaves into a religious nation. Moses led them across the Sea of Reeds and then to Mt. Sinai, where they participated in an awesome event which profoundly influenced the Jewish people and all of Western civilization. They gathered at the foot of the mountain, collectively experienced the presence of God, and came to understand that Moses was transmitting a set of laws that God expected them to observe. It was Moses who instructed them in the Ten Commandments, a basic moral code, as well as in all the other basic rules for a new religious society, but they understood that he was conveying God's will. God expected them to become a kingdom of priests and a holy nation.

Over the next forty years, as they wandered in the wilderness, they learned to organize and govern themselves. They became a proud, God-fearing people, finally ready to enter the Promised Land, Canaan, to live on their own soil.

When the community of Israel arrived at the Jordan River, Moses was succeeded by his disciple Joshua, who led his people in conquering and settling the land. Joshua did not take all of Canaan, but he succeeded in settling each of the twelve tribes in its own territory. For a while, these tribes maintained a separate existence without forming a united kingdom, but they banded together when threatened by an outside force and turned to outstanding individuals for leadership. These leaders were called Judges. The names of the most prominent Judges are Gideon, Deborah, and Samson.

In time, the need to stand up to threatening enemies required greater unity; the people demanded a king. The last of the Judges, Samuel, preferred to retain the existing system, but eventually acquiesced, and a promising young man named Saul was chosen as the first king.

Saul was different from other rulers of his day. Indeed, the kingship in Israel from its very inception differed from that of other nations. The king was not considered a divine figure in human form; he was not a potentate whose every word was obeyed unhesitatingly. Like all his subjects, the king was bound by the Torah and could never proclaim his will to be identical with God's. He was not God's representative on earth, nor was he the divine incarnate. Other members of the community formally represented religion: the priest *(kohen)*, who conducted the rituals, and the prophet *(navi)*, who boldly spoke out in the name of God against injustice. The great literary prophets first made their appearance in the eighth century B.C.E. They were men who were convinced that God had commissioned them to act as His spokesmen. They were His messengers, appointed to proclaim His divine will. They spared no one, whether monarch, priest, or fellow-citizen, who committed immoral or unjust acts. They insisted that justice and righteousness must prevail throughout all of society. The prophets taught that the Master of the Universe is concerned with what people do, and that God punishes those who lie to, cheat, or exploit others. They proclaimed morality rather than power as the decisive factor in world history; they demanded that spiritual love operate in human affairs. They called on their people to repent and turn aside from their evil ways, foretelling doom for those deaf to the message. They foresaw inevitable catastrophe as the divine punishment for wickedness. Yet, with all their fury and woeful warnings, they also promised future redemption and the ultimate return of the faithful remnant to an idealized Zion.

## The First Commonwealth

Saul did not fulfill the promise of his youth. Samuel was deeply disappointed in him, and consecrated David to take his place. After Saul fell in battle, David ascended to the throne. David's reign was filled with splendid achievements. He expanded the borders of Israel, and established a viable, powerful state. He captured the city of Jerusalem and made it the political and religious capital of his people. Generations later, the sages came to believe that the Messiah would be a descendant of King David (*Mashiah ben David*).

David's successor was his son Solomon, who built upon the brilliant achievements of his father. He introduced a new administrative organization that brought peace and prosperity to the kingdom. He built a central sanctuary in Jerusalem, a Temple which became the center for the worship of God. Moreover, Solomon encouraged writers who produced great literature. Some of the books of the Bible are attributed to Solomon or to his father. In later generations, Solomon was characterized as the wisest of all men.

The brilliant and accomplished court of Solomon, including an intensive building program, took its toll. It was achieved at the expense of burdensome taxes which the people found unbearably oppressive. As a result, an insurrection took place upon Solomon's death, and the united kingdom separated into two separate units. The Israelites to the north of Jerusalem, descendants of ten of the twelve tribes, set up a kingdom known as Israel. The two remaining tribes in the south constituted the kingdom of Judah. The northern kingdom was larger and wealthier, but its government was less stable. No dynasty remained in power very long. Established individuals took the crown for a short time only, since they or their offspring were assassinated and replaced by rivals. Israel entered into alliances with various neighbors from time to time, but these did not produce long-lasting benefits. The kingdom of Israel was conquered in the year 722 B.C.E. by the great empire of the day, Assyria. Some of the people must have escaped to the south or to neighboring lands. A few remained in the destroyed homeland. The majority, however, were carried off and dispersed throughout the Assyrian Empire, where they assimilated or died out. There are many legends about these "Ten Lost Tribes" but no one knows precisely what happened to them.

Judah was smaller, less affluent, and less prominent in international affairs. Ruled by the Davidic dynasty, the Judeans did not experience the frequent changes of regimes of their northern brethren but remained faithful to the king and to the Temple in Jerusalem. However, they could not withstand the onslaught of the Babylonians who succeeded the Assyrians as world conquerors, and to whom they lost their capital and sanctuary in 586 B.C.E. Many Judeans were taken into captivity. Unlike the Israelites, they were able to preserve their identity and did not disappear. They remained loyal to God even on alien soil.

The fall of Jerusalem and the destruction of the Temple did not have the same results as similar catastrophes among other ancient peoples. Others who lost independence and central sanctuaries soon ceased to exist. They accepted the superiority of their conquerors and assimilated. The Judeans, however, did not regard their disaster as a sign that the enemy possessed a stronger deity, but rather as God's punishment for their own sins. They did not attribute calamity to God's weakness but to His using the foe as His instrument. Moreover, they believed that Babylonia's arrogance and failure to recognize that she was only the rod of divine anger would lead to her own downfall.

The exiled community was a religious-national body the likes of which the pagan world had never seen. It remained loyal to God without cult, land, sacrifice, or temple. It even developed new institutions, such as the synagogue and prayer at fixed times. It attracted the attention of some who were accepted into the Jewish fold—the first religious conversions in history. People not born into the Jewish community were admitted into religious-ethnic membership and shared the conviction that all the nations would one day recognize and serve the one, true God. The prophet Isaiah taught his people that though they were derided and abused by the nations, they would ultimately be vindicated by a glorious redemption in which the glory of God would be revealed to all mankind. This was the beginning of Israel's impact on the heathen world.

The exiles never gave up yearning for Zion and praying for its restoration. When the Persian Empire replaced the Babylonian Empire after fifty years and King Cyrus granted the Jews permission to return, many returned.

## *The Second Commonwealth*

In 515 B.C.E., they rebuilt the Temple and proceeded to rebuild their religious-national lives. It was most difficult, and some became indifferent or faint-hearted. The scholar Ezra, along with Nehemiah, a gifted administrator, returned from Babylonia in the fifth century B.C.E. and unified the Judeans as a community pledged to the Torah. Some scholars regard Ezra as the editor of the Torah. He trained men to copy the sacred scrolls and to visit towns and villages to instruct the people and to explain the contents of the scrolls.

In the fourth century B.C.E., a new power arose on the world scene: the Greeks, led by Alexander the Great. As Alexander conquered the Near East, he spread the Greek way of life, known as Hellenism. He established Greek cities everywhere; his soldiers married local women; the Greek tongue became the language of civilized people; the Greek gods were worshiped. Pagan Hellenism with its poetry, art, sports, and glorification of the body, was very alluring. Most people succumbed to it. The Jews did not. Although there were Jewish Hellenists, the majority of the Jews in Palestine refused to surrender their faith in the one God or their own way of life. The contrast with Hellenism was striking. Judaism taught that spiritual strength was greater than physical power, that morality, not pleasure, should be the compelling determinant of individual and corporate action. The Hellenists did not perceive an ethical force at work in the universe. Judaism and Hellenism were too radically different for any marriage between them.

When Alexander the Great died, his empire was divided among his generals. Ptolemy became master of Egypt, while Seleucid became lord of Syria. Both claimed Palestine. As they fought each other, the rulers of the Jewish land often changed. Finally, in 198 B.C.E., the Syrian monarch succeeded in forcing Egypt to surrender Judea to him.

At first, the dominance of the Syrian Hellenists made little difference in the internal life of the Jews. They lived as they had before, without undue pressure to change their way of life. The High Priest served as their leader and was responsible to the government for order and taxes; teachers instructed students in Torah and met to deliberate religious matters. But this situation did not continue long, for the Syrians decided to force Helleni- zation upon the Jews. When, in 169 B.C.E., King Antiochus out- lawed the Sabbath, forbade circumcision, and sent troops to force the people to fulfill rituals of the Greek cult, a revolt erupted.

The banner of rebellion was raised by an elderly priest *(ko- hen)* named Mattathias and his five sons, who came to be known as "the Maccabees." His son Judah led his rebel followers in suc- cessful attacks upon the better-trained imperial soldiers. After three years, Judah the Maccabee and his men routed the Syrians and proceeded to cleanse the Temple so that the worship of God could be resumed there. The dedication (in Hebrew, *ḥanukkah*) and the cleansing ritual took eight days. Jews still celebrate *Ḥa- nukkah* as a festival marking the triumph of right over might, of the righteous over the ungodly. The Maccabean struggle was the first battle in history for religious freedom. *Ḥanukkah* is cele- brated annually as the anniversary of the rededication of the Temple rather than that of a military victory. It also celebrates the victory of Jewish tradition over Hellenism within the Jewish community.

The five Maccabean brothers all fell in the service of their people. Simon was the only one to survive the war. He presided over the peace and laid the foundations of the Hasmonean dy- nasty (*Ḥasmon* was the name of the family). Simon was assassi- nated in 135 B.C.E. and was succeeded by his son. Thus the children of the Maccabees became royalty seeking to establish and maintain national grandeur. They embarked on wars of conquest and soon came to resemble in many ways those whom their grand-parents had defeated. They adopted Greek names, pursued power, and became estranged from the masses and from Torah. Within less than a century, they lost their vigor and purpose—and eventually their crown.

By the middle of the first century B.C.E., the Romans controlled the region. When the great-grandson of Simon the Maccabee was deposed, the Romans installed a man named Herod on the throne. Although some historians speak of him as "Herod the Great," he is known in Jewish history as "Herod the Wicked." He was a brilliant administrator who built magnificent buildings and cities and headed an efficient army. Herod, however, was also a tyrant. He loved power more than he loved the God of Israel. He was not concerned with the welfare of his people, but was consumed by suspicion of those nearest to him, continually fearful of plots. Thus he put to death in-laws and friends, and even his own wife and sons. He died in 4 B.C.E., leaving Judea completely at the mercy of Rome. Upon his death, the Romans divided his realm among three of his surviving sons, but they proved so incompetent that Rome removed them within a decade.

Instead of appointing a new king, Rome ruled Judea directly, appointing governors over the province. These governors represented the worst features of colonialism. They were interested only in enriching their own coffers and were utterly insensitive to the needs, desires, and sensitivities of the people whom they ruled. They flouted Jewish religious law and cruelly enforced their will upon the populace. It was during the rule of one of the worst of the Roman governors, Pontius Pilate, that Jesus of Nazareth was put to death as a political offender.

The Jews, yearning for freedom and eager to break the foreign yoke, were increasingly irritated and outraged by the Romans. In the year 66, the Jews finally revolted. Despite inner dissensions, the Jews withstood the force of Rome for nearly four years. Rome, however, was a far superior military power. In the summer of the year 70, the Romans captured Jerusalem and destroyed the Temple. The day on which the Temple fell, the ninth day of the Hebrew month of *Av (Tisha B'Av)*, the very same date observed as the anniversary of the destruction of the first Temple, has remained a day of fasting and mourning.

Just as one might have expected the fall of Jerusalem and the destruction of the Temple in 586 B.C.E., to have brought an end to the Jewish people, so one might have expected the great catastrophe of 70 to have brought Jewish history to a close. Other peoples who suffered a similar fate soon ceased to exist. The Jews, however, did not disappear. Their leaders were able to transform Judaism into a powerful spiritual force that did not depend on a central sanctuary for national continuity. Subsequent Jewish vitality and creativity were rooted in the undertakings of those who supervised the shaping of Jewish life and thought following the tragedy: the rabbis.

One of the most distinguished rabbis, Yoḥanan ben Zakkai, managed to escape besieged Jerusalem before it fell. He sought out the Roman general Vespasian, whom he greeted as "Caesar." Shortly afterward, the Roman Senate elected that same general as Emperor. The new sovereign informed Rabbi Yoḥanan ben Zakkai that he would be granted a gift of his choice.

The sage asked for permission to establish a school in the small coastal town of Yavneh. He gathered the foremost scholars of the day to be with him there. They made Yavneh the spiritual and cultural center of Jewry. After the fall of Jerusalem, the rabbis in Yavneh were able to adjust Judaism to new realities. They laid the foundation of what came to be known as Rabbinic Judaism.

## The Rabbinic Era

The rabbis set themselves the task of interpreting the Bible and applying it to daily life. Their work is reflected in the many volumes of the Talmud which became the foundation of all later Jewish thinking and living. This work is not easy to describe. It is the record of the thoughts, convictions, debates, and decisions of Jewish spiritual leaders regarding all aspects of life: family relations, business affairs, ethics and morality, worship and ritual. It was edited in about the year 500.

In a summary such as this, it is impossible to present the chief characteristics of the Talmud even briefly. It is difficult to describe it because there is no similar work to which it can be compared. It consists of 63 tractates, yet it is more than a collection of tractates. Rooted in the Bible, it is filled with biblical verses in discussions and it repeatedly cites the Bible as the authority for its decisions; yet it is neither a biblical commentary nor a legal code. It is encyclopedic in nature but it is not an encyclopedia. It is the product of many men and had an editor; yet it is not the work of any one individual or group of individuals. The Talmud contains many judicial cases, but it is more than a legal work; it contains the give-and-take of discussions and arguments as well as asides which seem to have nothing to do with the specific cases that initiated the discussions. It includes ethics, religious practices and liturgy, laws regulating personal, commercial, and agricultural life, community organization, and social welfare.

The sages of the Talmud regarded the Bible as the revealed will of God and therefore the basis of both action and belief. The Bible, however, could not possibly have covered every contingency. Moreover, it sometimes seems obscure or speaks in generalities. For example, it takes marriage for granted but does not spell out marriage rites. It provides for divorce but does not specify the procedures to be followed. It prohibits work on the Sabbath but does not state precisely what is to be considered work. Many of the rabbis' interpretations and applications stemmed from ancient traditions; others were answers to contemporary questions posed by people who wanted to know how to live in keeping with Scriptural principles. Some were decisions resulting from cases that had come before them, for they also served as judges. All of these discussions and decisions constitute the Oral Law.

The Oral Law was deemed sacred and binding, although not to the same degree as the Written Law. For this reason, there was a reluctance to commit it to writing. There was a feeling that it must continue as an oral tradition. With the passage of time, however, the accumulated oral material grew to massive proportions and eventually was in danger of being forgotten. Therefore, various rabbis made their own compilations. None of these, however, became universally accepted until one of the foremost sages, Rabbi Judah (called "the Prince") arranged and edited the Oral Law in a systematic, concise way. His compilation, the Mishnah, was completed in 210 C.E. and became accepted by everyone as authoritative, second in importance only to the Bible. The Mishnah did not present all the deliberations leading to final decisions. Its text was limited to the cases, usually presented with both majority and minority opinions.

After the Mishnah was edited, new situations arose, new conditions and experiences brought new problems. The Mishnah had to be interpreted, expanded, and adapted. It became the text studied in the great academies of Palestine and Babylonia. The time came when all those discussions had to be collected and edited. This took place in Palestine in about 400 and in Babylonia in 499. This supplement to, or completion of, the Mishnah is called *Gemara*. Both together constitute the Talmud. The Mishnah and the Palestinian *Gemara* are known as the Jerusalem Talmud, or the Palestinian Talmud *(Yerushalmi)*. The Mishnah and the Babylonian *Gemara* are called the Babylonian Talmud *(Bavli)*.

The *Gemara* is not as concise as the Mishnah. It includes everything the rabbis and their disciples had to say as a result of hearing a Mishnah cited—their reactions, explanations, and deliberations, stories that came to mind, references to other opinions or other sources. Therefore, the Talmud is not a work that can merely be read; it must be studied. One can say that it is a record of the attempt of Jewish spiritual geniuses to build a godly society.

## The Gaonic Age

By the time the Talmud was completed, great academies existed where scholars sought to apply its teachings to life. The leaders of these schools were recognized as the religious authorities of all Jewry. Because each bore the title of *Gaon* (*gaon* means "excellency"), the four hundred years between 600 and 1000 is known as the Gaonic Age.

This period was one of great transformation in the outside world, which presented challenges that demanded responses. A dynamic new religion, Islam, arose in the seventh century and quickly spread throughout the Mediterranean region. The Arab empire of the eighth and ninth centuries brought together the Persian, Hellenistic, Arabic, and Jewish cultures. An era of astonishing cultural and intellectual creativity ensued. In the midst of this attractive and open Islamic culture, many young Jews began to question their own religious heritage. It became necessary to present Judaism in a way that made sense to the intellectuals of the era.

The man who did this most admirably was the most renowned of all the *Geonim,* Saadia (882–942). A first-rate scholar, Saadia Gaon was a master of the Islamic, as well as his own, tradition. His book *Beliefs and Doctrines* was the first major philosophical treatise on Judaism, the earliest systematic presentation of Jewish beliefs and teachings. Saadia felt the need to prove that science and philosophy do not conflict with Judaism and that, to the contrary, they validate it. He argued that truth is one, though there are different sources of the one truth. One source is reason, the other is the Jewish tradition. Therefore, true reason must lead to truths of revelation. For Saadia, the Torah is revealed reason.

Saadia presented proofs for the existence of God and arguments for the observance of Jewish commandments, thereby exerting a profound influence on the thinkers of his day and all who followed. He pointed a way to find meaning in Judaism while being part of a changing world.

The *Geonim* did not abruptly cease to function at the end of the first millennium, but their influence gradually waned. This was due partly to the lack of outstanding personalities and partly to the fact that the center of Jewish life was shifting from Babylonia to Europe.

## The Golden Age of Spain

In the eleventh and twelfth centuries, Spain became one of the great dynamic centers of Jewish life. Jews had lived there long before that, indeed as early as pre-Christian days, but they reached the peak of their creativity as their culture came into contact with Islamic culture after the Muslims conquered Spain in the eighth century. The Muslims of this period were relatively liberal. They allowed non-Muslim communities considerable legal and religious freedom and permitted them to share in the flowering of science, philosophy, and poetry.

A remarkable period of creativity ensued. It is usually referred to as "The Golden Age of Spain." Many Jews were completely at home in Arabic as well as in Jewish culture. They wrote commentaries on biblical books and rabbinic works as well as philosophical treatises, poetry, and linguistic studies. In addition to rabbis, the leaders of the Jewish community were physicians, astronomers, and statesmen. A few were even generals.

Among these giants, two were towering. One was the greatest Hebrew poet since Biblical days, Yehudah Halevi (ca. 1085–ca. 1140). Halevi, a physician, wrote poetry in Hebrew and philosophy in Arabic. His secular poetry is delightful, his religious poems are magnificent. Halevi was the great Singer of Zion

who expressed the deepest yearnings and undying love of his
people for the Holy Land. Many of his religious poems have been
incorporated into the liturgy.

Halevi's philosophical masterpiece, *The Kuzari,* expresses
ideas and emotions basic to the Jewish people, together with the
presentation of his own mystical experiences. Halevi maintained
that all humanity forms a living organism, with the Jewish people as its heart and conscience. Since the Jews cannot fully perform their function of elevating all of humanity while on alien
soil, they must return to their own land, where they could again
attain prophetic stature.

The other giant produced by Spanish Jewry was Maimonides (1135–1204), also known by the initials of his name, *R*abbi
*M*oses *b*en *M*aimon: Rambam. The Rambam was the greatest
philosopher of the Jewish people. He was a noted physician
whose medical treatises still receive serious consideration. And he
was a master of Jewish law whose legal works (especially the
compilation entitled *Yad Haḥazakah,* or *Mishneh Torah*) are still
authoritative.

Maimonides was a distinguished rationalist whose philosophical work, *A Guide for the Perplexed (Moreh Nevukhim),* was
written to answer questions about Judaism raised by young intellectuals. Maimonides, like his tenth-century predecessor Saadia, was convinced not only that religion and reason do not
conflict, but that they corroborate each other. What appears to
be irrational is simply misunderstood. He devoted part of his
book to explaining the meanings of specific words and concepts.
Maimonides deeply believed in God but did not attempt to define Him, pointing out that we can assert only what God is *not.*
Yet Maimonides also presented arguments to prove the existence
of God.

Despite his rigorous rationalism, Maimonides believed that
there are truths which reason cannot attain. They can be known
only by revelation. Maimonides believed that God reveals Him-

self to mortals even though He is pure spirit with no physical form. Not every person, though, is capable of experiencing this revelation. A few gifted individuals are endowed with the ability to receive communications from God. They are blessed with a gift that is superior to human reason.

The *Guide* is the greatest philosophic book produced in Judaism. Although much of it is now outdated, it nevertheless points to a method that can still be used. Maimonides did not deal with the specific problems of the twentieth century, but he struggled with problems so similar that he still serves as a guide for those who live so much later under such different conditions.

After Maimonides, the "Golden Age" began to fade. In the first half of the thirteenth century, the Christians drove the Muslims out of Spain, and would not tolerate other non-Catholic minorities. The flourishing cultural life of the Jewish community was harshly stifled. The Jews became subject to increasing discrimination and repression. They continually were pressured to convert and were threatened when they refused. Those who succumbed were watched constantly, suspected of living secretly as Jews. Frequently, the Jews were forced to choose between conversion and exile. Finally, they were expelled from Spain in 1492. From that time on, no Jew could openly practice Judaism in Spain until the middle of the twentieth century.

## European Jewish Communities in the Middle Ages

As Jews from Babylonia who fled persecution settled in Spain, so Jews from Palestine went to Italy, France, and Germany. From France, some Jews followed William the Conqueror into England.

The Italian Jewish community, one of the oldest in Europe, produced a number of scholars and other authors, but it never reached the heights of Spanish Jewry. Jews lived in England from 1066 until the expulsion in 1290. Legally, they were not permitted to return to England for four centuries. Jews were expelled from France in the fourteenth century and were not reestablished there until the eighteenth. At times in these communities, great scholars arose who left an indelible imprint upon all of subsequent Jewish learning.

French Jewry produced one of the greatest Jewish thinkers, Rabbi Shlomo Yitzḥaki, better known as Rashi (1030–1105), the commentator *par excellence* on the Bible and the Talmud. Ever since his day, these sacred texts are rarely studied without his commentaries. His straightforward, brilliant explanations clarify the most difficult passages. There is hardly an equal to Rashi in any other literature. Moreover, he trained disciples who supplemented his commentaries, not merely explaining words and passages but also developing Jewish law to meet contemporary needs while continuing the traditions of the past.

Rashi and his students lived through the terrible days of the Crusades. Enormous numbers of those who embarked on the Crusades, inflamed by religious leaders, were adventurers and vagabonds who hoped to become rich or who sought to avoid paying their debts. They were motivated more by financial gain than by religious fervor and were so eager for spoils that they could not wait to reach the Holy Land for their rampages. Violent anti-Semites among them ruthlessly attacked the Jews in France and Germany, massacring entire Jewish communities and leaving any survivors destitute.

In the twelfth century, Jews were accused of deliberately beating or stabbing the wafer used in Communion, causing it to bleed. This ludicrous charge of "Desecrating the Host" served as the justification for further attacks, murders, and agony. Another preposterous canard with the same horrible results was the Blood Libel, the accusation that Jews annually killed a Christian, whose blood was then purportedly used in the baking of *matzah*. These two lies spread throughout medieval France and Germany, causing unimaginable sorrow and torture. In the middle of the fourteenth century, Jews were blamed for causing the Black Plague, and were persecuted once more.

Life in Central Europe became so unbearable that great numbers of Jews decided to leave. Many settled further East, where there was promise of relative calm and tranquility. They were welcomed in Poland and Lithuania, which had been primitive and undeveloped before the thirteenth century. The leaders of those areas thought that the Jews, with their talent and experience, could help to develop their lands. The Jews lived up to the royal expectations. For a few generations they were granted many privileges and lived without undue harrassment. Toward the end of the fourteenth century, however, the situation changed. Fanatic clergy began to preach virulent hatred of Jews, and German Christian merchants who had followed the Jews to Eastern Europe now regarded them as undesirable competitors. The Jews were soon denied the right to live where they pleased. In the early fifteenth century, they were confined to very limited quarters. Privileges earlier granted to them were often rescinded. In 1555, Pope Paul IV ordered that the Jews be segregated in their own quarter. Subsequently, the Jewish Quarter everywhere came to be known as a "ghetto," a word derived from the Italian *geto*, which was a foundry in Venice near which the Jews lived.

The Jews nevertheless continued to thrive, and Polish Jewry reached its zenith in the following few centuries. The Jews were able to minimize the anti-Semitism of both Church and government, as well as to make a success of their financial ventures. They created a strong communal organization and enjoyed a remarkable degree of self-government, with their own courts, their own educational system, and their own administrative institutions. Local communities elected representatives to regional bodies and these bodies elected representatives to meet with those of other regional councils. Thus, the "Council of the Four Lands" came into being in the middle of the sixteenth century, constituting a virtual Jewish parliament. The council enacted laws governing taxation and business life, regulated social affairs, acted as a court of appeals, and supervised education and religious life.

The intellectual life of East European Jewry was on a remarkably high plane. Since the Jews were not welcome in the general society, and since the intellectual life of the general society was not very attractive, the Jews concentrated on the Jewish classics. Their educational system centered on the Bible, Talmud, commentaries on these documents and other religious works, and the intense study of Jewish law, not on mathematics, philosophy, or science. There was virtually no illiteracy among the Jewish men of Poland and Lithuania. Their great academies produced distinguished rabbis and other scholars. Learned men were found in practically every community. The universal reverence for learning created an intense spiritual and intellectual life even for those who occupied menial positions.

## Suggested Readings for Further Study

Eban, Abba, *My People* (New York: Behrman House and Random House, 1968)

Noveck, Simon, *Great Jewish Personalities,* vol. 1 (New York: Farrar, Straus and Cudahy, 1959)

Potok, Chaim, *Wanderings* (Philadelphia: The Jewish Publication Society, 1978)

ADDITIONAL SUGGESTIONS

Adler, Morris, *The Talmud* (Washington: B'nai B'rith, 1955)

Avi-Yonah, Michael, and Kraeling, Emil G., *Our Living Bible* (New York, Toronto, London: McGraw-Hill, 1962)

Bamberger, Bernard, *The Bible: A Modern Approach* (B'nai B'rith Hillel Foundations, 1955)

Heschel, Abraham J., *The Prophets* (New York: Harper and Row, 1962)

Montefiore, C.G., and Loewe, H., *A Rabbinic Anthology* (New York: Schocken Books, 1970)

Orlinsky, Harry M., *Ancient Israel* (Ithaca, N.Y.: Cornell University Press, 1954)

Sachar, Abram Leon, *History of the Jews* (New York: Alfred A. Knopf, 1965)

Schwartz, Leo W., editor, *Great Ages and Ideas of the Jewish People* (New York: Random House, 1956)

Trepp, Leo, *A History of the Jewish Experience* (New York: Behrman House, 1973)

# CHAPTER 9

# History: Modern Times

*T*HE stability of the Jewish community in Eastern Europe that
  enabled the Jews to develop their intellectual pursuits was
soon dealt a severe blow.

## The Early Modern Period

Calamity struck the Jews of the southern part of Eastern Europe
in the middle of the seventeenth century. A Cossack leader named
Chmelnitzki led a revolt in 1648 against his people's Polish land-
lords and ruthlessly struck out against their agents, the Jews. In
that year, and in the following year, Chmelnitzki's men brutally
tortured and killed thousands of Jews. Women were raped, ba-
bies were dashed against walls, and men were put to the sword.
Many Jews were sold into slavery, and all underwent terrorizing
experiences. Those who survived were physically and emotionally exhausted and financially ruined. The atrocities initiated by
Chmelnitzki continued for a decade. In some parts of the Ukraine,
entire Jewish communities completely disappeared; in others, only

one-tenth of the Jewish population survived. Refugees spread throughout Europe bearing terrible tales of woe and martyrdom. Neither the Church nor the government extended any protection or evinced the slightest concern. The blow was so severe that the Jews of the southern part of Eastern Europe were never able to regain their former economic and intellectual eminence.

In the 1660s, thousands of Jews throughout Europe were aroused from despair by a Turkish Jew, a mystic named Shabbatai Zevi, who claimed to be the Messiah. People who believed that the hour of redemption had arrived stopped doing business, in the expectation of being transported miraculously to the Holy Land. Many questioned the need to continue religious practices. Representatives from Jewish communities all over Europe made their way to his court and treated him as royalty. The excitement and agitation, the disruption of economic life, the talk of an end to this world, all led the Sultan of Turkey to order Shabbatai Zevi to cease his activities. The Sultan gave the self-styled Messiah the choice of death or conversion to Islam. When Shabbatai Zevi chose to convert, masses of Jews were plunged into despair. They were able to find consolation only in mysticism. Reason and logic could neither explain their plight nor assuage their distress.

It was not long before the rise of a powerful movement which brought spiritual comfort and inspiration to the despondent, impoverished Jews of Eastern Europe. It was called Ḥassidism (the word is derived from the Hebrew *Ḥassid,* pious one). Rabbi Israel ben Eliezer, better known as the *Baal Shem Tov* (1700–1760) founded this radical new movement.

Many legends are told about him, all reflecting a man of extraordinary spiritual depth. He taught the masses that they matter to God. He preached the intrinsic value of every human being, insisting that even the sinner contains goodness. He held that God is to be worshiped in joy and enthusiasm, that prayer is as precious as study. Thus he directed his people's righteous emotions into a deep and satisfying worship of God.

The disciples of the *Baal Shem Tov* were remarkable spiritual personalities who spread their versions of the master's doctrines throughout Eastern Europe. Those who followed them as disciples took the name of Ḥassidim. They lived with an intense faith in a God of goodness and love who is to be worshiped and served with goodness and love. At times, Ḥassidism degenerated into obscurantism; at other times it ascended to the rarefied air of mysticism. It has continued to be a dynamic movement within Judaism to our own day.

Not all Jews viewed the rise of Ḥassidism with favor. Particularly those in Lithuania, who had not suffered from the catastrophe that had struck southern Poland and were therefore able to pursue their studies with ardor, fought the new movement. These people were called *Mitnagdim* (derived from the Hebrew word *mitnaged,* an opponent). Their foremost spokesman in the eighteenth century was the phenomenal scholar Rabbi Elijah of Vilna, better known as the Gaon of Vilna (1720–1797). The Vilna Gaon's life was completely devoted to learning. He knew the Bible and the Talmud by heart; he studied philosophy, anatomy, and astronomy. He pored over manuscripts, discovering the correct readings of words whose transmission had become corrupted over the centuries. He explained and commented upon texts, he rendered decisions in matters of Jewish law. He emphasized that the way to serve God is through study, that study is a way of worship. And he became the personification of Rabbinic Judaism in his time. He could not accept a movement which stressed the emotions and minimized the intellect. The Gaon regarded Ḥassidism as a departure from the traditional emphasis upon learning, as an unbecoming emotional outburst which could easily lead its followers from strict observance of the law. His followers continued his opposition to Ḥassidim. The bitterness between the two camps eased only toward the end of the nineteenth century, when both joined hands to combat non-Orthodoxy and assimilation.

## Eastern European Jewish Life

At the end of the eighteenth century, the Kingdom of Poland was too weak to maintain itself. It was partitioned by Russia, Prussia, and Austria, with the area most heavily populated by Jews coming under the Russian crown. Russia did not want the Jews from the new area infiltrating Russia proper and therefore restricted them to the areas in which they had lived before the partition. This territory, known as "The Pale of Settlement," was further reduced in the nineteenth century. Since Jews were forbidden to move outside the Pale, they were forced into an economic straitjacket.

As the years passed, the suffering of the Jews increased. Each succeeding Tsar enacted laws that made life for the Jews ever more unbearable. The limited avenues for earning a living were constantly narrowed. Jews were frequently expelled from their villages and forced into the overcrowded cities of the Pale. In the middle of the nineteenth century, Russians drafted Jewish boys for a twenty-five year period of military service. Recruiters who did not fill their quotas would kidnap young boys from their homes. The autocratic rulers resorted to various ruses to convert Jews and reacted with anger when their attempts were frustrated. The Jewish masses remained stubbornly loyal to the faith of their ancestors. In the latter part of the century, Jews were victims of vicious attacks, called "pogroms," usually staged with the government's approval if not actually organized by the authorities. Until the end of the Tsarist regime, the Jews were treated with contempt and barbaric cruelty.

One can only stand in amazement at the tenacity with which these Jews maintained their high religious and cultural standards. They did not become vagabonds. They did not react to life with pessimism. They continued to regard learning as sacred and illiteracy as disgraceful. They were terribly poor, but their family life was warm and meaningful. Their moral standards remained high, and their communal institutions functioned effectively. Phenomenal scholars and great leaders emerged from these communities. Despite the hatred and suffering which they endured, they persisted in maintaining their faith in God, and lived a remarkably rich spiritual life.

## *Modern European History*

Some Jews in the nineteenth century examined their people's situation critically and concluded that the time had come to alter traditional patterns. Enthralled with European culture, they hoped to transform their "benighted" brethren into Europeans. The doctrine that they preached was called "Enlightenment." They were certain that civil rights would be conferred on Jews as soon as they adopted "enlightened" ways. Because they wanted to be just like everyone else, they worked eagerly for liberal causes.

This naive faith in the humanitarianism of non-Jews, however, was shattered by the Russian pogroms of 1881. They then saw that the most progressive of the Gentiles either participated actively in the looting and killing of Jews or, at best, were indifferent. Some Jews who nevertheless persisted in their optimism concluded that although Russia held no future for Jews, there was a viable future elsewhere. Hundreds of thousands emigrated to the West, particularly to the United States. A small group concluded that Jews must forge their own destiny in their own land. These forerunners of the modern Zionist movement provided support for those who went to live on the soil of Palestine.

Many Jews remained in Eastern Europe, and some of them welcomed the Communist Revolution. But the Jewish condition was not improved under the new regime. Anti-Semitism was declared illegal, but it persisted in the government and among the people. Although the Communists were atheists who deprived all religious groups of freedom, many were permitted to maintain contact with their coreligionists outside the Soviet Union. Not the Jews. The Jews officially were considered a national minority, but they were deprived of the rights granted other minorities.

When the Nazis marched into Russia they massacred thousands of Jews in addition to killing other Russians, but the Russian government later refused to acknowledge the unique tragedy of the Jews. Moreover, native Lithuanians and Ukrainians often aided the Germans in finding and murdering Jews. Jewish institutions were closed, and the communal structures which had served the community were forbidden. After World War II, the Soviets did not destroy Jews in pogroms as their Tsarist predecessors had done, but they inflicted great suffering on the Jews and forbade them to have relationships with Jews outside the Soviet Union. In the 1960s and 1970s many Jews were able to leave (for either Israel or the United States), but the possibilities for migration were rendered almost impossible in the 1980s.

The miserable and humiliating conditions of Eastern European Jews in Tsarist times were not to be found in Central and Western Europe. Ever since the French Revolution, legal disabilities gradually had been eliminated. The Jews still were not accepted as true equals, but they were not as legally isolated as they once had been. Anti-Semitism continued to be virulent, but was neither as crude nor as flagrant as in Eastern Europe. Jews of the late eighteenth and early nineteenth centuries were admitted into citizenship and could participate in the general culture.

The greater democracy of nineteenth-century Western Europe brought Jews many rights long denied them, yet did not grant them complete equality or complete acceptance. For two years the French Parliament debated the question of equal rights for Jews before deciding to grant them. Not long afterward, Napoleon limited the emancipation by decreeing for Jews humiliating laws which would not be repealed for decades.

If not legally, then socially Jews were often looked upon as outsiders by their fellow citizens. Still they were grateful for their new status and took advantage of the new opportunities. Indeed, many Jews gained distinction and eminence in cultural, academic, and political spheres. Some members of the Jewish community were so enchanted with general society that they became superpatriots prepared to surrender nearly everything in their own tradition.

The successful assimilation of French Jews into the national culture, however, did not inhibit anti-Semites or deter hatred of Jews. In 1895, few Frenchmen objected when Captain Alfred Dreyfus was disgraced and imprisoned on the trumped-up charge of selling state secrets to the Germans. He was chosen to take the blame for the misdeeds of others solely because he was a Jew.

French Jewish life was not as intensively Jewish as that of Eastern Europe. Prominent Jews were active in philanthropy and in defending Jewish rights. Adolphe Crémieux (1796–1880) was an important political leader who gave of his time and exceptional ability to protect his fellow Jews. In the following generation, Baron Edmond de Rothschild became the patron of the colonists seeking to rebuild Palestine. But in general, the French Jewish community had few scholars and lacked vigor, creativity, and vibrancy.

This could not be said for Germany, although at the beginning of Emancipation it seemed as if the Jewish community would soon cease being viable, so intoxicated were Jews with the promise of integration into Germany society. Moses Mendelssohn (1729–1786), one of the foremost philosophers of his day, taught that Jews could become part of German culture and also adhere to the Jewish tradition. His children and disciples, however, were committed only to the former. All but one of Mendelssohn's own sons converted to Catholicism, including Abraham, father of the composer Felix Mendelsohn. In the beginning of the nineteenth century, many Jews converted in order to become completely accepted into the general community.

Many others, however, took steps to stem the exodus. Some wrote about the treasures of the Jewish past in a way that could be appreciated by their contemporaries. Others sought to adjust Judaism to the new situation by declaring it to be only a religious faith. By negating the national and folk aspects, they expected Jews to be accepted as merely one more religious denomination on the national scene. They created the Reform movement as an attempt to adjust Judaism to a radically new situation and were able to check the flight from Jewish ranks of those who wanted to become part of German society.

Reform was not the only response of Jews who wanted to share the benefits of Emancipation while refusing to surrender their past. Some upheld a new kind of Orthodoxy, one which combined strict adherence to Jewish law with participation in general culture. Still others insisted that Jewish law, which they recognized as binding, has its own mechanisms of adjusting to new situations, and held tenaciously to the national aspects of Judaism. They were the forerunners of Conservative Judaism. Reform, modern Orthodoxy, and Conservative Judaism were all born in Germany as Jews reacted to the new conditions presented by the nineteenth century.

In the twentieth century, German Jewry produced seminal thinkers who exerted a profound influence upon modern Jews. The writings of Hermann Cohen, Franz Rosenzweig, Martin Buber, and Leo Baeck sparked a renewed positive identification with Jewish values and the Jewish people. Tragically and cruelly, the advent of Hitler spelled doom for German Jewry and rendered it virtually nonexistent in the contemporary world.

British Jewry was also part of the West, but its development was unlike that of its counterparts on the continent. Equal rights and citizenship were not suddenly thrust upon the Jews of England; they were enjoyed long before they became legal. Jews began returning to the British Isles in the late seventeenth century and quickly became part of English life without surrendering their heritage. Not until the middle of the nineteenth century was the last vestige of legal discrimination removed, allowing Lord Rothschild to take his seat in Parliament. But British Jews had been free of the kind of stress and strain characteristic of the French and German struggles for acceptance.

Although British Jews were formally Orthodox, and Reform made little headway, the Jewish community of England was not exceptionally pious, nor did it produce outstanding thinkers and scholars. Sir Moses Montefiore was an important figure in international Jewish life. He gave tremendous sums to help Jews in the Holy Land and elsewhere, and traveled great distances to plead the defense of his brethren. His name was revered throughout the Jewish world, and countless institutions were named "Montefiore" in love and appreciation.

To be sure, there were anti-Semites in England as elsewhere, but they were never powerful enough to endanger Jewish life and well-being. After 1881, many refugees from Tsarist oppression settled in London or elsewhere in the British Isles. They brought with them Yiddish culture and traditional piety. As they adapted to England and to British ways, they surrendered some aspects of their traditional way of life. They did not, however, rush headlong into new patterns that required complete abandonment of the old. They adopted the general British conservatism and formalities while preserving their identity with their fellow Jews.

## Anti-Semitism

Throughout the centuries, Jews have been scorned and oppressed in every country where they have lived. Unfortunately, modern enlightenment has not eradicated hatred of Jews. Although much of the world reacted with horror to the Nazis' genocidal and methodical murder of millions of Jews, many people still accept and act upon anti-Semitic ideas. The Soviet government refuses to allow Jews the freedom to study and practice their religion and limits the opportunities of Jews to participate fully in society. Western anti-Semitism today is more subtle, less harsh, but still persistent. Throughout the world, fanatics occasionally and indiscriminately kill Jews.

There is no one cause of anti-Semitism. It is a complex phenomenon rooted in religious, social, political, economic, psychological, and cultural factors. Analyzing them is not completely satisfying, but it can help us to understand the disease and it may point to ways of combatting it. We must remember, however, that the convinced anti-Semite is indifferent to truth and facts. Jews have been accused of such contradictory things that one wonders how any sane person could accept the charges. Jews have been labeled ruthless capitalists and radical socialists, rootless internationalists and rabid nationalists, culturally sterile and dominating the creative arts. Although Jews have not had enough power even to save their own lives, they have been charged with plotting an international conspiracy to overthrow all governments. Perhaps nothing indicates the psychic aberration of anti-Semites as clearly as these ludicrous libels, but the tragic truth is that they have been believed by too many.

Probably the most powerful source of anti-Semitism for the past two thousand years has been the Christian denunciation of Jews as Christ-killers. There was some religious distrust and dislike of Judaism even before the birth of Christianity; some pagans could not understand ethical monotheism and refused to acknowledge as valid a religion which insisted that God cares about all human beings, that He demands compassion and justice, that He asserts the triumph of right over might. Those pagans, however, have passed from the world scene. As Christianity grew, it increasingly turned against its parent and accused Jews of the worst of evils. Because Jews refused to accept the new doctrines, they were held guilty for the death of Jesus. No one stopped to consider the utter illogic of a charge which denied the very foundations of the new faith. If Jesus indeed died on the cross to atone for humanity's sins, then the crucifixion was part of God's plan and a blessing; on the other hand, if that death resulted from human stubborness, then it was not for humanity's welfare and was not from God. Here, however, as in all anti-Semitic propaganda, one must not expect logic or reason.

Because of the virulence of religious anti-Semitism, we

should probe the historical record more deeply. We need to remember that crucifixion was the *Roman* method of putting a
prisoner to death; hundreds of thousands met their end at the
hands of the Romans in this cruel fashion. Secondly, the Jews in
Judea could not have executed anyone even if they had wished to
do so, for their Roman rulers never granted them such authority. Moreover, Jesus had done nothing against Jewish law to
warrant any kind of judgment. His offense was against Rome.
Jesus was nailed to the cross by order of the despotic Pontius Pilate, who considered Jesus to be politically dangerous.

This historical fact was distorted in the years that followed.
Leaders of the Catholic Church, including popes and bishops, and
Protestants like Martin Luther, insisted that the Jews be punished for their rejection of Christian teachings. Jews have always
been astonished and outraged by the hostility of people who state
that their religion is based upon love, who act violently in the
name of a gentle Jesus.

One analysis of this form of anti-Semitism was presented by
Maurice Samuel in his book, *The Great Hatred*. He contends that
the Christian's accusation that the Jews killed Jesus is a cover-up
for a deep spiritual problem. He asserts that the Jews were hated
because they were Christ-*givers*. The pagans, even as they converted, resisted Christianity's call for morality. They turned on
Jesus, the Jew who had set forth ethical imperatives for them.
They remained Christians while rejecting Christ.

Only in our day have Christian religious leaders denounced
the cruelties and agonies caused by teachings of the past, and
urged their fellow Christians to repent. Pope John XXII was one
such leader. Under his direction, Vatican Council II officially declared that neither the Jews in Jesus' day nor their descendants
are to be held accountable for his death. Other Catholic spokesmen, such as the late Cardinal Spellman of New York and the late
Cardinal Cushing of Boston, vigorously denounced anti-Semitism as sinful and un-Christian. The renowned Protestant theo-
logian Reinhold Niebuhr affirmed the legitimacy of Jewish

existence and called for an end to all attempts to convert Jews. Some Protestant bodies have also declared anti-Semitism a sin and are seeking ways to remove all vestiges of it. Lutheran leaders in 1983 denounced Martin Luther's anti-Semitism.

Nevertheless, despite official pronouncements, anti-Semitism has not disappeared. This places a serious responsibility upon church bodies. Some Christian groups commendably have revised passages in their textbooks and in their liturgy, so that their adherents are not indelibly impressed with negative images of the Jew. They will have to explain sections of their Scriptures in light of historical circumstances so that the attitudes adopted because of a specific encounter or event are not taken as models. Religious anti-Semitism today is certainly not as vocal or as virulent as in centuries past, but as long as it persists it is a denial of what Christianity teaches as well as a danger to democracy.

Not all anti-Semitism stems from religious teachings. Jews were often disliked because of their role in economic life. Anti-Semites projected the image of the Jew as a Shylock, a crafty moneylover who could not be trusted. Often this was simply a projection of their own characteristics. Non-Jews who loved gold more than virtue, who broke their word when it paid to do so, who charged enormous rates of interest for loans, attributed these failings to the Jews. In medieval Europe, agriculture and non-commercial avenues of earning a living were forbidden to Jews, who then were accused of failing to enter these very occupations.

Non-Jewish merchants were more hostile to their Jewish competitors than to those who were not Jewish. When there was prosperity, they tolerated Jews; when conditions were difficult, they sought to be rid of them. Indeed, this pattern has persisted to the present—when conditions are good, prejudice is at a minimum; at times of depression, it becomes more active.

Some hate-mongers have insisted that the Jews have a defect in their blood, that the Jews are an inferior, degenerate race. These racial theories were reflected in the national policy of the Third Reich when the Hitler government embarked upon a program of exterminating those whom it declared to be genetically inferior. One hesitates even to respond to the inanities about "the Jewish race" but, because gullible people have accepted that theory, it is necessary to point out that people of many races are Jews. Most of the racial nonsense disappeared with the defeat of the Nazis, but it continues to crop up occasionally.

At times Jews have been selected as the object of derision because of their minority status, as a minority in every land and a majority in none. The awareness that this lack of status engendered fear and degradation led many Jews in the past several decades to Zionism. They concluded that anti-Semitism could never wane until the Jewish people ended their exile to become once again a people with a national home.

Such views were closely related to those which recognized that many men and women generally dislike that which is different; indeed, they often fear it. It takes considerable maturity to realize that differences are good rather than evil, that every group has something distinct to contribute to the totality, and that uniqueness does not contradict amity and brotherhood. Unfortunately, many people have not yet attained that maturity and continue to look upon other groups with suspicion if not hostility.

## Sephardi and Oriental Jews

The history sketched in these pages has been that of the Jews in Europe and the United States. Jews, however, have lived all over the globe. Jewish communities have existed in North Africa and in the Middle and the Far East for millenia. They are mentioned in biblical sources, and their numbers increased after the fall of both Temples (the First in 586 B.C.E. and the Second in 70 C.E.). The Jews accepted the culture of the people among whom they dwelt, yet they maintained their own identity, were loyal to their own religion, and remained loyal to the homeland in Judea. Although they often suffered discrimination and persecution, they maintained their high intellectual and spiritual standards.

Particularly after the First Arab Conquest in the seventh century C.E. in Egypt and in the rest of North Africa, the Jews were usually considered legal and social inferiors. Yet they produced outstanding sages and scholars for many centuries. The renowned Rabbi Saadia Gaon was born and reared in Egypt; Moses Maimonides practiced medicine in Cairo; first-rate scholars lived in what is today Morocco, Tunisia, and Algeria. The communities declined in the Middle Ages, but they did not disappear. The Jews lived in their own quarters (called the *mellah*), usually in squalor and poverty. They followed and maintained their traditions faithfully. After the birth of the State of Israel, most of them went to the homeland.

When the second Temple fell, some Jews undoubtedly fled south to Arabia. By the fifth and sixth centuries, there were powerful Jewish tribes in southern Arabia. Some even succeeded in establishing a Jewish kingdom. When Muhammed started his new religion in the seventh century, he appealed to the Jews to join him. Some did, but the majority refused to do so. Until 1948, small Jewish communities were able to maintain themselves. The largest was in Yemen, where Jews were treated with contempt and harshness, but nevertheless maintained schools and produced scholars. After 1948, the community was transported to the newly established Jewish State.

The area known today as Iraq and Iran was called "Babylonia" in ancient times. Nearby Syria was home to some Jews even before the beginnings of Christianity. Foreign conquerors came and went without putting an end to the Jewish community. Despite their deprivations and sufferings, these Jewish communities produced poets and scholars. In the present century, persecution intensified and most (but not all) left Syria for Israel. Those who have remained have no rights and are subject to cruel discrimination.

Until the eleventh century, Babylonia was the center of

amazing creativity. The Talmud was completed there in 499; for nearly five hundred years, the *Gaonim* flourished as leaders and scholars in rabbinic studies, philosophy, biblical commentary and other fields of learning. The center of Jewish life gradually passed to Europe after the year 1000 but the Jews of Babylonia enjoyed long periods of tranquility. The situation changed with the coming of the Mongols in 1258, followed by the Huns and later the Turks. Academies of learning continued to exist but they did not compare with those of former days. With the passage of time, Jewish life deteriorated, especially after Iraq became independent in 1932. Whoever could leave after 1948 did so.

Iran is also a Muslim land although it is not generally considered part of the Arab world. The majority of the population belongs to the Shiite branch of Islam, less tolerant of differences than the Sunni which is dominant elsewhere. Under their rule, Jews often experienced persecutions, expulsions, and forced conversions. Still, the literary output of Iran's Jews was rich and their Jewish loyalties strong. In the nineteenth century, their condition grew worse and they suffered from ignorance and poverty. Their situation improved somewhat under the last shah but it became more precarious than ever under the Ayatollah Khomeini.

Long ago, some Jews of Iran ventured further east to do business in India, where they found Jews who maintained that their ancestors had arrived in biblical times, claiming descent from the Ten Lost Tribes. All that is definitely known about their origin is that they have lived in or near Bombay since the Middle Ages. These Jews had accepted the idea of caste from the general environment. They had forgotten Hebrew and used the native Marathi language instead. They were brown-skinned, had no contact with Western Jews, and observed some religious practices (circumcision, dietary laws, and the Sabbath). They did not intermarry with "white Jews" and maintained their own communal life. After 1948, many went to Israel where they encountered problems in being accepted as full Jews. It was not until

1964 that the Chief Rabbis of Israel ruled that the Bene Israel from India are legally Jewish.

On the southwest coast of India, in and near Cochin, was a community of Black Jews. It is presumed that they were offspring of converts who probably had been slaves of Jewish settlers. The Cochin Jews had no contact with the rest of world Jewry for centuries. The local rulers generally treated them with tolerance; in 1957, the rajah gave them a site near the palace for a synagogue. The Cochin Jews wore native dress and spoke the native tongue, but they prayed in Hebrew and zealously followed Jewish law. After 1948, most of them emigrated to Israel.

The third group consists of Jews who came to India from Iraq in the early nineteenth century and considered themselves superior to the local Jews. They held themselves aloof and did not intermarry with them. They established their own synagogues and schools, and had little to do with their coreligionists who had long been in India. Many of this community also moved to Israel and, for many years, retained their bias against the Bene Israel and Cochin Jews.

Jewish traders of Iran also traveled to China, and some settled there. When Turks stopped the trading in the sixteenth century and old caravan routes fell into disrepair, Jews living in China became isolated. There is little reliable information about Chinese Jews, although there are stone tablets from Kaifeng, capital of the Chinese Empire in the tenth through the thirteenth centuries, as well as later inscriptions. In 1461, flood waters from the Yellow River destroyed Torah scrolls and most of the Kaifeng synagogue. The Jews of the city then obtained Torah scrolls from other communities in China (a tablet erected in 1663 mentions thirteen Torah scrolls). Over the course of time, knowledge of Jewish history was forgotten and intermarriage increased, yet some traditions were maintained. A Protestant missionary in 1866 found only a few thousand Jews there, and they soon assimilated. It is believed that a few Jews survive in Kaifeng, but the government does not allow outsiders to contact them.

In the 1840s, a number of British Jews settled in Shanghai. Not long afterward, a number of Russian Jews settled in some Chinese cities. During World War II, many refugees from Hitler were able to reach Shanghai and to establish a Jewish community. Most, however, left after the war and only a handful of Jews are to be found there today.

Jews did not come to Japan until it was opened to the world in the nineteenth century. Those engaged in business were restricted to a few cities (as were all foreigners) and made no effort to establish a Japanese Jewish community. The only Japanese Jews today are the few who have converted and married Western Jews. The small Jewish community in Tokyo is made up mainly of Western Jews.

The communities mentioned here have remained part of the Jewish people, servants of the God of Israel, though most accounts of Jewish history refer to them rarely, if at all. Ashkenazi Jews may have looked upon them as somewhat exotic, but never questioned their kinship. There even have been groups, such as the Jews of Ethiopia, who were cut off from the main Jewish body for centuries, to be reunited only in our day. The Jewishness of Jews who had been isolated in some parts of India for a long while was once questioned by Iraqi Jews. The religious authorities in the State of Israel, however, eventually declared them to be *bona fide* Jews. The Jewish people have been scattered in many countries, but even small groups of Jews separated from the mainstream tenaciously have held on to their faith and identity. The sense of unity of the Jewish people has overcome the divisions into Ashkenazim and Sephardim and Orientals. This has been made explicit in our day by their ingathering in the State of Israel.

## Suggested Readings for Further Study

MODERN TIMES

Dawidowicz, Lucy, editor, *The Golden Tradition: Jewish Life and Thought in Eastern Europe* (New York, Chicago and San Francisco: Holt, Rinehart and Winston, 1967)

Noveck, Simon, *Contemporary Jewish Thought* (Washington: B'nai B'rith Books, 1985)

Sachar, Howard, *The Course of Modern Jewish History* (Cleveland and New York: The World Publishing Company, 1958)

### Additional Suggestions
Dawidowicz, Lucy, *The War Against the Jews, 1933–1945* (New York: Bantam, 1976)

Heschel, Abraham Joshua, *The Earth Is the Lord's* (New York: Henry Schuman, 1950)

Wiesel, Elie, *Souls on Fire* (New York: Random House, 1972)

ANTI-SEMITISM

Gade, Richard E., *A Historical Survey of Anti-Semitism* (Grand Rapids, Michigan: Baker Book House, 1981)

Hay, Malcolm, *Europe and the Jews: The Pressure of Christendom on the People of Israel for 1900 years* (Boston: Beacon Press, 1960)

Prager, Dennis, and Telushkin, Joseph, *Why the Jews?* (New York: Simon and Schuster, 1985)

### Additional Suggestions
Forster, Arnold, and Epstein, Benjamin R., *The New Anti-Semitism* (New York: McGraw-Hill, 1974)

Isaac Jules, *The Teaching of Contempt* (New York, Chicago and San Francisco: Holt, Rinehart and Winston, 1964)

Parkes, James, *The Conflict of the Church and the Synagogue* (Cleveland and New York: The World Publishing Company, 1961)

———, *The Jewish Problem in the Modern World* (New York: Oxford University Press, 1946)

Poliakov, Leon, *The History of Anti-Semitism, vol. I* (New York: Schocken Books, 1974)

———, *The History of Anti-Semitism, vol. 2* (New York, The Vanguard Press, 1974)

SEPHARDI AND ORIENTAL JEWS

Chouraqui, Andre N., *Between East and West* (Philadelphia: The Jewish Publication Society, 1968)

Cohen, Hayyim, *The Jews of the Middle East*: 1860–1972 (New York and Toronto, Jerusalem: Israel Universities Press, 1973).

Patai, Raphael, *Tents of Jacob* (Englewood Cliffs, N.J.: Prentice-Hall, 1971)

Pollak, Michael, *Mandarins, Jews and Missionaries* (Philadelphia: The Jewish Publication Society, 1980)

Strizower, Schifra, *Exotic Jewish Communities* (New York: Yoseloff, 1962)

# CHAPTER 10

# American Jewish History

$T$HE New World, particularly that part of the North American continent which became the United States of America, was developed by people of varied national and religious backgrounds. Although a particular group may have become a majority in a certain area, none was exclusive; minorities and ethnic differences always have been a fundamental part of American culture. In such a society, Jews were able to achieve a status denied them in Europe. There were anti-Semites who disliked Jews intensely, but they were looked upon with disfavor by the government and could not prevent Jews from sharing the freedom and other American blessings enjoyed by all. Indeed, the Jews have always been an important thread of the many-colored tapestry that has constituted American life.

Jews crossed the ocean to the New World with other European immigrants. They had problems in all areas controlled by Spain, for the Spanish had exported the Inquisition and the intolerance of non-Catholics wherever they went. Some Jews sought to hide their origins, for those who openly practiced their religion were declared heretics. Some were even burned at the stake. In 1531, the Dutch captured Brazil and allowed Jews the same freedoms offered to others. In 1654, however, when Portugal wrested Brazil from Holland, approximately five thousand Jews had to flee. Many recrossed the ocean to find a home in Holland or England; some settled in British colonies (such as Jamaica). One group of twenty-three Jews made their way to New Amsterdam (which ten years later fell into British hands and was renamed New York).

Although Peter Stuyvesant, governor of New Amsterdam, was not very cordial to the refugees, he obeyed the orders of his employers, the Dutch West Indies company, and allowed them to settle. Thus the first Jewish community in what is now the United States was established. The numbers gradually increased and they were granted certain rights, which were extended by the British. In 1655, the first Jewish congregation, Shearith Israel, was established. It still flourishes in New York City.

The second Jewish settlement was in Newport, Rhode Island. The other New England colonies, not hospitable to dissidents, extended freedom only to members of the established church. Pennsylvania was more liberal, and Jewish congregations existed there by the late eighteenth century. They were also established in Georgia and South Carolina, but other colonies in the south were not yet prepared to tolerate minorities.

The situation improved with the American Revolution and the Constitutional guarantee of equality for all. Although a few states did not agree to the separation of Church and State when they became part of the Republic, that principle was guaranteed by the Constitution. Nearly all the Jews sided with those who broke the ties with England and supported those who fought for independence. Haym Salomon, a Polish Jew who settled in Philadelphia and became a stockbroker, was known as the "financier of the American Revolution." At great personal sacrifice, he provided the desperately needed funds required by George Washington to maintain his army and the new government.

There was no large Jewish immigration in the early years of the Republic. The Jews in the country were citizens, and met with little overt discrimination; indeed, many assimilated. The majority of them were Sephardim, i.e., of Spanish ancestry. German Jews began coming in the third and fourth decades of the nineteenth century, many fleeing after 1848, when an attempt at revolution failed in Germany. The Jewish population, which numbered only 4,000 in 1820, grew to 50,000 in about twenty years and to 250,000 in 1880. These Jews (called Ashkenazim in contradistinction to Sephardim) were poor, hardworking people who had left everything for a new land that offered freedom to work and freedom to worship God in their own way. Whereas Jews who came earlier had settled in the East, many of these newcomers went inland, helping to settle the Midwest. Some went further, even as far as California. Many were pioneers who traded with Indians or provided other pioneers with supplies. Many were plucky peddlers who eventually settled and opened stores, thereby quickening the economic development of the country. A few founded establishments that grew into huge department stores (such as Macy's and Gimbel's in New York City). As these Jews found fellow religionists, they established congregations. The first synagogue in Cincinnati was founded in 1824 and a second in 1841; St. Louis's first congregation was established in 1836, Louisville's in 1824; by 1847, Chicago had one and it was not long before there were others in many towns and cities. As these pioneers prospered they remembered the less fortunate and created organizations to help new immigrants and to take care of Jewish welfare needs. They also founded hospitals, free loan societies, and fraternal orders such as B'nai B'rith.

By the time of the Civil War, Jews lived in both the South and the North, sharing the loyalties of their fellow citizens in those regions. Judah P. Benjamin was secretary of state for the Confederacy; other Jews were ardent Union supporters. One historian has identified six thousand Jews in the Union armies and twelve hundred in the Confederate.

The post-Civil War era was a time of building the institutions and movements that were to serve American Jews in the years to follow. Those seeking to remain loyal to the Jewish religion while adjusting it to American life embraced the ideology and patterns of Reform Judaism which had been brought over by German Jews. The principal organizer of Reform Judaism was Rabbi Isaac Mayer Wise (1819–1900) who, after a stay in Albany, New York, settled in Cincinnati, Ohio. His goal of organizing all Reform congregations became a reality in 1873 when the Union of American Hebrew Congregations was formed. In 1875, the Hebrew Union College, a seminary for training rabbis, opened its doors in Cincinnati with Rabbi Wise as president. In 1889, Rabbi Wise succeeded in organizing the Central Conference of American Rabbis, the professional organization of Reform rabbis.

The hope that American Jews would be united, not divided into separate schools, proved to be in vain. Reform Judaism rejected the binding authority of the Talmud and of Jewish law. Forerunners of the Conservative movement opened the Jewish Theological Seminary in 1886 to train rabbis according to *their* principles. In 1902 the renowned scholar Solomon Schechter (1850–1915) was invited to come from England to head that seminary. He began to develop institutions of the Conservative movement. In 1913, Schechter organized Conservative congregations into the United Synagogue of America. The alumni of the Jewish Theological Seminary organized the Rabbinical Assembly of America in 1901 to represent the Conservative rabbinate. In later years it accepted into membership qualified graduates of other rabbinical schools.

The Orthodox did not create institutions until later, when their numbers swelled with the large immigration of East European Jews between 1881 and 1914. There was no single personality who served as a central figure, and more than one rabbinical seminary, rabbinical organization, and congregational union emerged. The Orthodox have given great stress to Talmudic education, and have established several major *yeshivot* which ordain rabbis. The best known are the Isaac Elchanan Yeshiva in New York City, which is part of the expanded Yeshiva University, and the Hebrew Theological College in Chicago.

Biographies of prominent personalities are beyond the scope of this summary of American Jewish history. Yet, a few men and women who achieved fame as writers, philanthropists, and communal leaders must be mentioned. For example, Mordecai Manuel Noah (1785–1851) was a journalist and flamboyant playwright who served for a while in the consular ranks and even became sheriff of the City of New York. Noah dreamed of establishing a Jewish state on Grand Island near Buffalo, New York, which he purchased for that purpose. His scheme elicited little response, however, and nothing followed the grand spectacle which initiated the project.

Rebecca Gratz (1781–1869) was a charming Philadelphian who served as the model for Rebecca in Sir Walter Scott's *Ivanhoe*. She was a pioneer of Jewish Sunday Schools and devoted her talents to many projects helping her fellow Jews.

Rabbi Isaac Leeser (1806–1868) was one of the chief defenders of the Jewish tradition. He founded and edited an important Anglo-Jewish journal *(The Occident)*, translated the Bible into English, did pioneering work in Jewish education, and established a school which was the forerunner of the Jewish Theological Seminary.

Henrietta Szold (1860–1945), the founder of Hadassah, dedicated her remarkable talents to Jewish learning and to the redemption of her people. Rabbi Stephen Wise (1874–1949), the magnificent orator, fought for social justice in America, and for justice for his people everywhere, particularly in Zion. The eminence of Justice Louis Brandeis (1856–1941) in jurisprudence did not still his devotion to Zionism.

The majority of the Jews who left Eastern Europe after the terrible Russian pogroms of 1881 and 1882 came to the United States. A handful went to Palestine, and some went to Argentina

or to Western Europe. Until immigration to the United States
was stopped during World War I, hundreds of thousands came
annually. By the time they arrived, both the Sephardim and the
German Jews had become fully Americanized and looked on their
East European brethren as "greenhorns." Yet, with all their feeling of social superiority, they helped the newcomers adjust to
their new environment. In the 1880s, the Hebrew Immigrant Aid
Society (HIAS) was formed to assist immigrants in getting a start
in the new land. In some communities, settlement houses, the
forerunner of our contemporary Jewish Community Centers,
were developed. As the number of Jewish organizations grew,
leaders decided to cooperate in fund-raising and in serving the
entire community; they created Jewish Federations wherever there
was a sizable Jewish population. To help Jews overseas, the Joint
Distribution Committee was established early in the twentieth
century.

The Jews from Eastern Europe came from an environment
that was more intensely Jewish and less affected by the non-Jewish world than those from Central and Western Europe. Though
eager to become part of America, they held on to the Yiddish
language and did not readily surrender their religious culture.
True, many were so enthralled with their new freedom that they
cast aside all traces of their previous lives, but the majority retained their traditions and their way of life. As a result, a Yiddish
press and theatre prospered. Orthodoxy grew and several rabbinical schools *(yeshivot)* were founded. Many of these Jews went to
work in factories, often suffering under depressing and inhuman
conditions. Influenced by the prophetic tradition of social justice
and by the ideals of socialism, they became pioneers in trade
unionism and labor movements.

The offspring of these immigrants played important roles in
the general American culture as well as in the Jewish community. Some entered the theater and became the foremost actors,
entertainers, and writers of their day; some entered the academic
world and became renowned scientists and scholars; some en-

tered government service and occupied important posts; some became noted financiers or labor leaders. Within a generation, the children of the East European Jews were indeed at home in American society.

This did not happen without a struggle. The immigrants had to overcome extreme poverty and want. They had to cope with the problem of observing the Jewish religion in an environment that made observance extremely difficult. They had to face great intellectual and spiritual challenges. And they had to face anti-Semitism. Although it never erupted into the pogroms and massacres that were so characteristic of its European counterpart, it was blatant at times of stress and depression. Even in times of general prosperity it did not disappear from the land of opportunity and freedom.

In the 1920s there were Jews who thought that they could abandon their heritage, but within a few years the shock of Hitler brought most of them to an awareness of being part of the Jewish people. The interest in a Jewish homeland intensified and intellectuals began reaffirming their Jewishness.

Some elements in the community began to focus upon what could be done to counter anti-Semitism and to weaken the potency of that disease. Organizations were founded to defend the Jews, to work for laws that prohibit legalized prejudices, and to educate. Besides the national religious bodies, the most prominent are the American Jewish Committee, the American Jewish Congress, and the Anti-Defamation League of B'nai B'rith. Each emphasizes a different aspect of the war against bias and prejudice, but all are constituted to defend the good name of the Jew, to stop rumors, to safeguard legal liberties and to combat bigotry. Other organizations, such as the National Conference of Christians and Jews, endeavor to promote fellowship, and various religious groups, Jewish and non-Jewish, such as the Synagogue Council of America and the Catholic Conference of Bishops, foster dialogues and ecumenical understanding as well as specific programs to counter prejudice.

Some programs have proven to be inadequate and others have produced positive results. Half a century ago, some Jews believed that it was important to minimize their differences from the non-Jews. This idea has been repudiated, for it was both dishonest and futile. When Jews became carbon copies of their neighbors and yet did not convert, they were regarded as no different from the Jews who still maintained their distinctiveness.

Some have felt that Jews need only refute the lies told about them for anti-Semites to realize the error of their ways. This naivete has been dispelled with the increasing awareness that hatemongers are indifferent to truth and that all the proofs of their inaccuracies cannot alter their basic antipathy.

Many academicians are guilty of blind hatred and strong biases. This does not mean that lies should not be refuted or that education is in vain. People who are not emotionally disturbed, or who are neutral in regard to Jews, can be persuaded by the truth. Certainly children can be kept from developing unconscious antipathies by good textbooks and enlightened teachers.

The area of legal action is crucial as well. Laws do not change people's opinions, but they do prevent antisocial behavior. Moreover, legal decisions create new situations in which certain patterns of conduct become the norm. Therefore, while we recognize that laws prohibiting biased behavior may not change views and attitudes, they are necessary and must be pursued.

The most effective way to counteract prejudice and to minimize antagonism is person-to-person contact. People who get to know other people are more open to the recognition that all human beings are children of God. Meetings of people from different groups can do much toward establishing mutual respect and concern.

Leaders from various Christian groups and representatives of the Jewish community have been meeting often to explore the nature of both traditions, even though there are both Jews and Christians who disapprove of such dialogues. There are Christians who insist that Christianity is the sole path to God and that it is incumbent upon those who know the truth to bring others to that path. There are Jews who distrust all theological discussions with Christians and who are convinced that such meetings are masked attempts at conversion. Most Jewish and Christian spokesmen, however, are genuinely interested in mutual understanding, in sharing values without expecting others to convert to their faith. On local and national levels, such dialogues are very different from the superficial brotherhood gatherings of the past during which leaders annually would proclaim vague generalities. As true dialogues increase, the hope for acceptance of pluralism and for genuine harmony among those of different faiths and traditions comes closer to realization.

While many national Jewish organizations in early twentieth-century America defended Jewish interests in the United States and abroad, others, such as the various Zionist organizations, strove to gain support from non-Jews as well as from Jews for a Jewish State. Still others engaged in activities to strengthen and deepen the religious, cultural, and communal interests of American Jewry.

By the end of World War II, the distinctions between Sephardim and Ashkenazim and between German and East European Jews had all but faded; all had become American Jews. They had common leaders and institutions, common interests and needs, common problems and challenges. Together, they had to focus upon perpetuating Jewish values and living meaningful Jewish lives in an environment that reflected Christianity even when it was secular. Together, they had to find means and ways of improving and intensifying Jewish education. And together, they had to accept the responsibility of aiding and at times rescuing oppressed Jews in many parts of the world. The Jews of the United States no longer had to worry about physical survival, but they did have to be greatly concerned about fashioning an intellectual and spiritual Judaism worthy of the heritage transmitted from the past.

There are pessimists who do not believe that they can succeed. They consider the forces making for assimilation to be overwhelming. They foresee the gradual disappearance of all Jewish communities outside of Israel and argue that a contemporary meaningful Jewish life can be lived only in a predominantly Jewish environment. They, however, are a minority. Most American Jews feel that Judaism can not only survive but can be creative and dynamic even as a minority faith. They recognize the huge problems, the urgent need to provide quality education and to transmit significant religious teachings, but they insist that the problems can be solved. There is nothing inherent in American culture that would prevent a flowering of Jewish culture. The fate of Jewish culture and faith depends upon the commitment of American Jews.

## Suggested Readings for Further Study

Howe, Irving, *World of Our Fathers* (New York and London: Harcourt Brace Jovanovich, 1976)

Lebeson, Anita, *Pilgrim People* (New York: Harper and Brothers, 1950)

ADDITIONAL SUGGESTIONS

Feingold, Henry, *Zion in America* (New York: Hippocrene Books, 1974)

Glazer, Nathan, *American Judaism* (Chicago: University of Chicago Press, 1967)

Karp, Abraham, *Golden Door to America* (New York: Viking Press, 1976)

_____, *Haven and Home: A History of the Jews in America* (New York: Schocken Books, 1985)

Liptzin, Sol, *Generation of Decision* (New York: Bloch Publishing Company, 1958)

Sklare, Marshall, *The Jewish Community in America* (New York: Behrman House, 1974)

CHAPTER **II**

# Zionism and the
# State of Israel

$A$ LTHOUGH the Land of Israel has been a holy land for Christians and Muslims as well as for Jews, there is a significant difference. Christians never thought of it as "the Land of Christianity," nor did Muslims venerate it as "the Land of Islam." Both groups have regarded certain places and shrines there as sacred, and important figures in both religions have had some association with the land. To Jews, however, the Land of Israel *(Eretz Yisrael)* is more than a place where important religious events once took place, and more than the site of past national independence. For Jews, it has always been the only place where they could fully assume their responsibilities as a people of the Lord. It is the source of their being and the land of their destiny. For centuries, Jews believed what the Prophets taught—that only after they were restored to Zion and peace was established would all people beat their swords into plowshares and enjoy universal harmony, love and righteousness.

There has always been a Jewish community in the Holy Land, though it has been small at times. Jews have included it in their daily prayers wherever they have lived. Regardless of the climate wherever they have lived throughout the world, they have prayed for rain when the rainy season was due in the Land of Israel. Three times a day their prayers repeated: "May our eyes behold Your return to Zion" and "Rebuild Jerusalem, Your holy city." After every meal, they voiced their yearnings for return to the Holy Land. Passages in the wedding ceremony recall Jerusalem and the Land.

Poets and philosophers throughout the ages have been eloquent in expressing the deep love of the entire people for *Eretz Yisrael*. For centuries, however, the Jews did little about returning in great numbers, and there were no large scale back-to-Palestine movements. People relied on God to answer their prayers for the speedy realization of the Messianic promise.

By the second half of the nineteenth century, social and political conditions in Europe created a climate that changed this passivity to activism. Italy and Germany, swept by strong nationalist movements, became autonomous states. The revolutionary ideas of Darwin and other scientists spurred the intelligentsia to reject the supernatural bases of religion which had encouraged passive resignation. The increased virulence of anti-Semitism and the persecution of Jews stimulated many young men and women to reject the traditional role of martyrdom and to initiate activities which would radically alter the status of their people.

The first movement to direct the age-old yearnings for Zion into activities that would lead Jews back to *Eretz Yisrael* came into being after the pogroms of 1881–82. This movement, called *Ḥibbat Tziyon* (Love of Zion), did not enroll many members but it did elicit widespread support. Moreover, it succeeded in starting the modern Jewish settlement of the historic Jewish homeland. The *Ḥibbat Tziyon* movement, considered dangerous by the Russian authorities, had to carry on its activities clandestinely. Chapters were formed; speakers traveled across the Pale of Settlement to deliver speeches; articles and pamphlets aroused Jews to seek a return to Zion. The members collected funds to support the courageous ones who actually left Russia to establish colonies in the ancestral homeland. They also established and supported schools and published journals which became vehicles of the new idea.

The leaders of *Ḥibbat Tziyon* not only urged the colonization of Palestine, they also pioneered the revival of Hebrew. Although the national tongue had never died out, it had not developed much linguistically after the Middle Ages.

Perhaps the best representative of *Ḥibbat Tziyon* goals was Asher Ginzberg, who is better known by his pen name, Aḥad Ha'am (1856–1927). Aḥad Ha'am was a master Hebrew stylist who taught that the characteristic which binds all Jews, past and present, is ethical nationalism. (Since the word "nationalism" now has a political connotation which it did not necessarily convey half a century ago, we might well substitute the word "peoplehood.") He did not oppose the idea of a Jewish state, but did not regard it as an immediate objective. Political Zionists sought Jewish autonomy. Aḥad Ha'am envisioned a Jewish community reborn in *Eretz Yisrael* as a spiritual center which would revitalize and influence all Jews wherever they lived, no matter what the size or population of the community in Israel. Because of his emphasis on this role of a Jewish national entity and his key role in reviving Hebrew literature, Aḥad Ha'am became known as "the Father of Cultural Zionism."

An even more popular nationalist philosophy at the end of the nineteenth and beginning of the twentieth centuries was "Political Zionism." The "father" of this movement was Theodor Herzl (1860–1904), a Viennese journalist who once had advocated assimilation as the answer to the Jewish problem. After Captain Alfred Dreyfus was found guilty of treason in France simply because he was a Jew, Herzl came to the realization that Jews could never lose their identity. The Dreyfus trial caused Herzl to conclude that anti-Semitism was a deep and ineradicable disease throughout Christendom. Herzl's solution to the

Jewish problem was a Jewish State, to be granted political legitimacy by the great powers of Europe. He convened the first Zionist Congress in 1897 to launch the World Zionist Organization.
Herzl's charismatic personality and the grandeur of his vision attracted Jews throughout the continent and elsewhere. Whereas
*Ḥibbat Tziyon* was engaged in small-scale projects and did not
embrace all of Jewry, Zionism was all-embracing and placed the
Jews on the international agenda. This movement persevered despite setbacks, indifference and even betrayal, until it finally
achieved the establishment of the State of Israel in 1948. Since
then, Zionism no longer has had the same political functions but
has assumed other tasks which assist and strengthen the Jewish
state.

In addition to "Cultural Zionism" and "Political Zionism",
there was a third type which exerted the greatest impact on those
personally engaged in the task of rebuilding. It was called "Labor Zionism" because it insisted that the new Jewish Commonwealth had to be built by the personal labor of Jews. It called for
Jews to return to the soil from which they had so long been ban-
ished by their oppressors in the Diaspora. It represented a join-
ing of Socialism and Zionism, an insistence upon a just and
equitable society in which there would be no exploiters and no
exploited. Some Labor Zionists were Marxists, and others advocated the kind of equality preached by the Prophets, but all
believed in the importance of manual labor and a return to agriculture.

The pioneers who resolved to put their theories into practice were not trained for their task. They had not been reared on
physical labor; they were not familiar with the climate and diet
of *Eretz Yisrael*; they knew little of the Arabs with whom they had
to interact. Nevertheless, they proceeded with undaunted spirits.
They dried up swamps, built roads, planted and weeded and cultivated. They revived a land which had been neglected and bar-
ren for ages. And, as they did so, they resolutely revived the
Hebrew langauge and created a vibrant cultural life.

The three different aspects of Zionism remained distinct before World War I, but there were those who saw them as a part of a whole and spoke of "synthetic Zionism." The man who coined that term was Dr. Chaim Weizmann, the brilliant scientist who was a loyal disciple of Aḥad Ha'am, a friend of Labor Zionists and president of the World Zionist Organization in the twenties and for much of the thirties. During World War I, Weizmann succeeded in convincing the British Government of the justice of the Zionist cause as well as the benefits which would be Britain's by being its sponsor. The British committed themselves in the Balfour Declaration of November 2, 1917, which stated that "His Majesty's Government looks with favor upon the establishment of a Jewish national home in Palestine." That promise received formal, legal authorization a few years later when the League of Nations entrusted Great Britain with the Mandate over Palestine.

The Mandatory Government was faced with the very difficult problem of reconciling Zionist interests with those of growing Arab nationalism. British officials thought that they could curb Arab extremism by a policy of appeasement. London was concerned with imperial interests and sought to maintain the loyalty of the Arab world, even at the expense of promises which had been made to the Jews. Therefore, Arab rioters were neither suppressed nor punished. Whenever the Arab leadership fomented disturbances, restrictions were imposed upon the Jews. The Arabs' contention that the growing Jewish population frightened them resulted in a limitation on Jewish immigration. The argument that Jews were acquiring too much land led to restrictions on land purchases. The early Zionists bought land from Arabs who own large tracts of land.

The Zionist enterprise succeeded despite the vitriolics of Arab spokesmen and despite the indifferent or inimical colonial officials in Great Britian. The leaders had great faith in Britain's sense of honor, in her democratic traditions, in her general philo-Semitism. They were discouraged but not despondent as a result of the increasingly anti-Zionist positions she adopted. Reluctantly, they accepted the partition of Palestine in 1922, which established Arab rule in the section east of the Jordan River. (It was first called "an emirate." In 1948, it became the Hashemite Kingdom of Jordan.) Later, Dr. Weizmann and his colleagues were prepared to accept various plans to divide western Palestine since they felt that having any sovereign territory was better than being subject to the whims of outsiders. The Arabs, however, refused to accept any partition plan. The United Nations finally was forced to declare the partition operational without their endorsement, in November of 1947.

Early in the Mandatory regime, the Jews learned that they could not rely on British troops to protect them against murderers and terrorists. They therefore established their own self-defense corps, the *Haganah*. The *Haganah* was a disciplined fighting force responsible to the Jewish authorities. It refrained from terrorist acts, even from reprisals, but defended Jewish life and property from attacks. Even when the British would not permit refugees fleeing from Hitler's horrors to enter Palestine, the *Haganah* refrained from taking the offensive against Arabs or Englishmen. Continual provocation, however, led a minority to reject the *Haganah* philosophy in favor of a more activist policy. They believed that only Jewish military action could stop Arab aggression and force the British to leave. They organized themselves into a separate military organization, known as the *Irgun*.

British policies before World War II were not as oppressive or as intolerable as they were after the war. Despite immigration quotas, all kinds of Jews did come: religious and nonreligious, capitalists and socialists, farmers and city dwellers. The cities—New Jerusalem, Tel Aviv, and Haifa—expanded, and small towns developed. The kibbutz movement, founded in pre-World War I days, established collective agricultural settlements. Other kinds of cooperative settlements emerged too. The Hebrew language became the vernacular. The Hebrew University in Jerusalem and the Haifa Technion, which had opened their doors in the mid-twenties, expanded. Hebrew dailies and journals reflected vibrant and creative thought. The theater, art, and the Palestine Symphony Orchestra were all part of a sophisticated cultural life.

During this period, the Jews developed their own democratic structure in order to govern themselves. They formed political parties reflecting their varied ideologies, and these parties elected delegates to an Assembly of Representatives. That Assembly and its executive, the National Committee *(Vaad Leumi)* conducted all the affairs of Palestinian Jewry. The parties also elected representatives to the World Zionist Organization, thereby sharing in the decision-making policies of their colleagues who were not in *Eretz Yisrael*. When the State of Israel came into being on May 4, 1948, the Jews were well prepared for a smooth transition from running a semiautonomous community to a national government.

The state came into being because Great Britain could no longer continue to exercise the Mandate. On the one hand, Arab leaders grew increasingly intransigent, demanding far more territory than what British leaders were prepared to give. On the other hand, the British were not willing to implement the creation of the Jewish national home. Despite their best efforts, however, they were unable to prevent the "illegal" immigration which was dramatically increasing the Jewish population of Palestine.

During this period, the terrible disclosures of the Nazi atrocities made the nations of the world keenly aware of their obligations to the Jewish people. The United Nations concluded that partitioning Palestine was the only solution to the thorny conflict. The decision was taken on November 29, 1947. The Mandate ended on May 16, 1948.

In the intervening months, pressure was put on the Zionists to refrain from proclaiming a state. The leader of Palestinian Jewry, David Ben Gurion, refused to acquiesce. On the day preceding the British withdrawal, he and his colleagues met to proclaim the birth of the State of Israel. Ben Gurion became prime minister, head of the government; Chaim Weizmann was elected president, an office that was mainly symbolic; a parliament *(Knesset)* of 120 members was created. The new democracy began to function without delay.

Immediately, immigrants began pouring into Israel by the hundreds of thousands. None were turned away, even though the infant state was embroiled in a war of survival. The Arab states, members of the United Nations, refused to abide by the majority decision and declared a war of annihilation. They were vastly superior to the Jews numerically, yet were unable to defeat Israeli determination. In 1949, Israel was finally able to defeat the foe. Under pressure from the United States and the Soviet Union, and with the United Nations' promises to safeguard the borders, Israel withdrew from conquered territories and hoped for peace.

Peace, however, continued to be elusive. Many Arab leaders declared their determination to throw the Israelis into the sea. Backed by Russia, they became increasingly aggressive, threatening the very existence of Israel. The Six Day War broke out in June of 1967 and resulted in an amazing victory for Israel. Israelis reunited the Old City of Jerusalem with the New; captured the Golan Heights, from which Syrians had often fired at Jewish farmers and fishermen below; and took Sharm-el-Sheikh, the point which controlled free passage into the Gulf of Aqaba and hence shipping to and from the port of Eilat.

The Israeli Army occupied the Sinai peninsula, the Gaza Strip, and the area west of the Jordan River that had been taken by Jordan in 1948.

This victory still did not bring peace. The Arab leaders continued to vow eternal hatred and revenge. Terrorists were trained to infiltrate and to kill Israeli civilians. The United Nations was unable to impose any restraint. And then on Yom Kippur, in October of 1973, Egypt and Syria attacked again. Though caught by surprise, the Israelis were able to win yet another military victory. But they were unable to make any political progress. They paid a terrible price in the loss of lives and in psychological insecurity. It was hoped that peace would emerge from the new situation, but the Arab countries persisted in looking upon Israel as their implacable foe.

Among Arab leaders, only Anwar Sadat of Egypt concluded that continued warfare was destructive for everyone. With amazing courage, in defiance of the rest of the Arab world, he went to Jerusalem in 1979 to initiate a peace process. This trip, which electrified the world and instilled hope in the hearts of many people, was soon followed by the Camp David meeting which concluded with a peace treaty between Egypt and Israel. President Carter, President Sadat, and Prime Minister Begin were able to overcome what had seemed insurmountable problems and to inaugurate a period of peace between the most important Arab country and the State of Israel. The other Arab governments condemned Sadat, expelled Egypt from their organizations and tried to isolate it economically and politically. They entered the 1980s without altering their basic positions, although some of them from time to time seem to be more conciliatory.

The imminent dangers threatening Israel from its very first hour could easily have led to a totalitarian regime. Such changes occurred in many other states created after World War II, states that were much less threatened than Israel. Israel, however, has remained steadfastly democratic. Elected officials are responsible to the electorate through their parties (similar to the British rather than the American system). Freedom of speech, freedom of the press, and freedom of religion are part of the fiber of life for Israeli citizens. Religion does play a role that is absent in Western democracies, for each religious group has exclusive jurisdiction over marriage and divorce of its adherents. All public institutions are closed on the Sabbath and Festivals, and follow the Jewish dietary laws. Stores and businesses are closed on Saturday and there is no public transport in most places on that day. Since the builders of the state and those of Near Eastern origin did not know about the attempts to adjust the Jewish religion to western culture and knew little about the Reform and Conservative movements, religion became synonymous with Orthodoxy. Moreover, there was an Orthodox political party in the World Zionist Organization from the beginning of the century and it became part of the political arrangements when the state was born. As a party, it made demands in the area of religious life in return for its political support which was needed to form a ruling coalition. After the birth of Israel even the non-Zionist Orthodox formed a political party and won concessions when they were needed for a coalition. Thus, the Orthodox became part of the Establishment and had their way in religious matters. The Reform and Conservative movements in Israel are still small and must struggle against those who would deny them legitimacy as a religious tradition. Most synagogues are Orthodox, but Reform and Conservative congregations are slowly developing. The latter are not mere replicas of their American sister congregations, and will undoubtedly come to represent an indigenous non-Orthodoxy. Non-Orthodox rabbis are not permitted to officiate at marriages or to carry out the functions that are theirs in other countries, but they and their movements are struggling for the acceptance of religious pluralism in Israel. It should be noted that, even though non-Orthodox Jews are not granted religious equality, freedom of religion is extended to non-Jews living in Israel.

The development of Israel would not have been possible without outside help. Jews throughout the world have been deeply conscious of their responsibility to guarantee the successful survival of the state. The United Jewish Appeal annually collects millions of dollars; the Israel Bond Organization sells millions of dollars worth of bonds for investments; the Jewish National Fund collects large sums for reforestation, land reclamation, and development. Thus, a partnership has existed between the Jews in Israel and their brethren elsewhere. This partnership is more than financial. Whereas the Jews of the Diaspora contribute funds, they receive great psychological, cultural, and spiritual benefits in return. All Jews benefit from the existence of the State of Israel. Instead of the image of the Jew as a poor, oppressed refugee, there is now one of a proud, free, liberty-loving people. Literature, the arts, and drama have flourished, vastly increasing Jewish creativity. In Israel, Jewish civilization is primary. The Bible has come to life again and its values have been incorporated into daily life. The vision of Aḥad Ha'am is on the way to becoming a reality. Israel has already become a cultural center for all Jewry, imbuing Jews with new purpose and new life. One who looks at the total picture is often reminded of the old song: *Am Yisrael Ḥai,* The People Israel Lives!

## Suggested Readings for Further Study

Gilbert, Martin, *Exile and Return* (Philadelphia and New York: J. P. Lippincott Company, 1978)

Sachar, Howard, *A History of Israel* (New York: Alfred A. Knopf, 1976)

ADDITIONAL SUGGESTIONS

Eban, Abba, *My Country: The Story of Modern Israel* (New York: Random House, 1972)

Elon, Amos, *The Israelis: Founders and Sons* (New York: Bantam, 1971)

Heschel, Abraham Joshua, *Israel, An Echo of Eternity* (New York: Farrar, Strauss and Giroux, 1967)

Litvinoff, Barnett, *To the House of Their Fathers* (New York, Washington: Frederick A. Praeger, 1965)

Rubenstein, Aryeh, editor, *The Return to Zion* (Jerusalem: Keter, 1974)

Samuel, Maurice, *Harvest in the Desert* (Philadelphia: The Jewish Publication Society, 1944)

# CHAPTER 12

# *Judaism and Christianity*

JUDAISM and Christianity have much in common because both are founded upon faith in the one God of the Bible. Both regard the Hebrew Bible as sacred. Both uphold the sovereignty of God and the unity of humanity. Both are dedicated to love, compassion, truth, and justice. Yet these and other cherished values held in common do not minimize the real differences that do exist. These differences do not mean that one is superior to the other or that one must be antagonistic to the other. Each provides meaning for its adherents, and each must do so without disparaging the beliefs and practices of the other.

Jesus and his followers were loyal, devout Jews. They did not conceive of themselves as otherwise. They were totally devoted to the God of Israel and to the Torah of Israel. They observed the religious laws of their people, and spoke their language. They followed the customs and usages of Israel, and fashioned their thought in terms that stemmed from the traditions of the Jews.

How and why did Jesus and his disciples become the foundation of the Christian Church? The study of history cannot provide the complete explanation of the Church's development, but it does provide important background for a fuller understanding.

Scholars have not reached unanimous agreement about many facts and interpretations, but their works provide valuable insights. They give us a better idea of the socio-political and economic conditions of the era, the religious beliefs of the Jewish people, and the effect that assimilating into Greek civilization had on non-Palestinian Jews. We will attempt to sketch an outline of the historical background of the early stages of Christianity.

As far as anyone can tell, and there is no clear-cut evidence, Jesus was born in the year 4 B.C.E. This was the last year of King Herod, whose rule of nearly forty years in Judea had tyrannized and improverished his subjects. On the one hand, Herod was a most capable administrator and a great builder; on the other, he was a despot who suppressed all dissent and was much more of a Roman than a Jew. Herod had become King of Judea by decree of the Roman Senate. He was never regarded by his Jewish subjects as one of them. His fear that legitimate claimants might remove him from the throne led him to put many people to death, including his own wife and sons. Keenly aware of the Judeans' feelings about him, Herod prohibited political discussions and all public gatherings.

The severe oppression which characterized Herod's reign did not ease with his death. His sons and heirs were even worse, and Rome finally removed them from their positions of power. The Roman governors who ruled directly were colonial officials of the worst sort. They made no attempt to improve the lot of the people they governed, but filled their own coffers and used their troops to suppress any kind of protest. One of the worst was Pontius Pilate, a cruel and rapacious governor who was utterly indifferent to the religious and cultural practices of the Jews.

Economic as well as political conditions of this period were insufferable. The privileged few were becoming richer, and the masses were becoming poorer. Nature also seemed to be working against them; an earthquake and a famine had made their lot even more miserable.

What were the Jews to do? Had they been pessimistic by nature, they might have resigned themselves to an evil world, to wait passively for its end. But as heirs of biblical tradition they could not view the universe negatively. Although present conditions were miserable, they believed that the future would be better. Some Jews became political activists and conspired to overthrow Rome. Others looked only to Heaven for help. Some allowed their imaginations to run wild, as apocalyptic literature attests. But even nonextremists were convinced that God would not allow His people to perish. They expected the imminent arrival of the Messiah, a divinely sent emissary who would bring about national redemption and universal peace.

Some people banded together in small sects to follow their own interpretations of the Jewish religious tradition. The Dead Sea Scrolls, discovered in the 1940s, describe the beliefs of the Essenes, one small monastic sect. But such groups had relatively few members.

The dominant religious and political groups were the Sadducees and the Pharisees. Because members of these groups have been incorrectly depicted in the Gospel narratives, and because these groups evoked the allegiance of most Jews in the period we are considering, it is important to understand them and to point out the differences between them.

The Sadducees were the party of the aristocrats, the priests, and the affluent. The Pharisees were the party of the masses. They differed not only in their political and economic views, but also in their religious positions. Both accepted the Torah as the sacred text which reveals God's will. They differed over the matter of authority. Who had the authority to interpret the Torah and to decide how its teachings should be applied? The Sadducees insisted that only the priests possessed this authority; the Pharisees held that this was the task of those sages who studied and mastered all of traditional learning, not those who were priests by virtue of birth.

The question of authority involved more than democracy. The Sadducees held to the letter of the law, precisely what had been written down. They refused to accept the continuing development of the law which characterized the Pharisees' approach. The Sadducees tended to interpret the law strictly and harshly, while the Pharisees tended to be more flexible in their interpretation.

For example, the Torah teaches: "An eye for an eye, a tooth for a tooth" (Exodus 21:24). Today, we know enough about the ancient world to appreciate what an advanced step this was by comparison to other people for whom the penalty could be death, or who could exact unequal penalties based upon the social positions of offender and offended. Thus, the Torah's law was a giant step toward true justice. The Pharisees, however, regarded the literal meaning of the verse to be unacceptable. They insisted that the Torah never intended this law to be taken literally, that it really refers to appropriate compensation. The person responsible must pay damages to the victim, including compensation for time lost from work and for any shame or embarrassment that had been incurred.

The Pharisees, interested in the masses, stressed the biblical teaching that the entire Jewish people constitutes "a kingdom of priests and a holy nation." The Sadducees were more concerned with the privileged classes. The Pharisees believed the soul to be immortal; the Sadducees denied both resurrection of the dead and reward and punishment in the afterlife, because these doctrines are not stated explicitly in the Torah. The Pharisees believed that all people are children of God; the Sadducees insisted that God's love extended only to the Judeans.

The Pharisees were concerned mostly with the synagogue; the Sadducees, with the Temple. The Pharisees survived the destruction of the Second Temple in the year 70 C.E. Their teachings became the basis of the subsequent evolution of Judaism. The Sadducees disappeared after the destruction of the Temple, when the priesthood came to an abrupt end.

It is obvious, then, that the picture of the Pharisees in the Gospels is inaccurate, and that the negative connotation of the word "Pharisee" to designate a narrow-minded, rigid legalist as it is understood by many even today, is not based on historical truth. It may be that the authors of the Gospels, displeased that the Jews refused to acknowledge Jesus as the Messiah, blamed their stubborness on the sages who led the Pharisees.

In all likelihood, Jesus himself was a Pharisee. If he indeed said what he is quoted as having said, he was rebuking those Pharisees who were not being true to Pharisaic teachings.

In this discussion it is also important to take note of the Jews who lived outside of Palestine. Jewish communities had long existed in Alexandria, Rome, and Asia Minor. They adhered to their ancestral faith with devotion and sent contributions to the Temple in Jerusalem, but their language was Greek and they were also part of the Greco-Roman world. This did not necessarily dilute their commitment to Judaism. At the same time, the ethical ideals of their tradition attracted many pagans who were repelled by the immorality and degeneracy of paganism. Relatively few of these actually converted to Judaism; most of them found circumcision and the dietary regulations too great a burden. Nevertheless, they felt drawn to a God of justice and righteousness, to a faith which taught the sanctity of every human being, to a religion which preached love and compassion.

These people were known as "God-fearers." They probably had become familiar with some Scriptural teachings through the Greek translation of the Bible (known as the Septuagint). This translation, however, opened the door to some misconceptions.

For example, the Hebrew word for a young woman was erroneously translated into a Greek word for virgin. The Hebrew word for God was translated into a Greek word for a pagan god.

The Hebrew word *Torah* was translated into the Greek word for law, thereby leading to the misrepresentation of Judaism as rigidly legalistic. The problem was not limited to the translation of words which failed to convey the meaning of the original. The meaning of many Jewish concepts also suffered in translation. This paved the way for some of the mixing of Jewish and Hellenistic ideas which took place in the time of the early Church.

Very little is known about Jesus. We have no biography written by those who knew him personally. Contemporary records do not mention him. Neither Jewish nor non-Jewish documents of the era refer to him directly. Those who loved him, however, told stories about him which were transmitted verbally. By the time they were written down, they had been embellished. Many of the versions and the oral traditions do not agree with each other. Thus, the Gospels which seek to tell about the life of Jesus often contradict each other or are not consistent with historical realities. Moreover, the Gospel writers apparently did not intend to write objective studies. They composed religious tracts as men of faith seeking to transmit a picture of Jesus as the Christ, rather than as the Jew of Nazareth. Despite the enormous difficulty of reconstructing the accurate record, it is possible to get some idea of Jesus' career and teachings.

He was raised in the Galilean hills, in the city of Nazareth, far from the turmoil and sophistication of Jerusalem. He received some sort of Jewish education, and was familiar with the Torah, the psalms and some rabbinic teachings. As a young man, he came under the influence of an itinerant teacher, Yoḥanan (John the Baptist), who declared that the long awaited period of the Kingdom of God was at hand. Jesus became a wandering preacher and faith-healer who attracted devoted followers. He did not preach anything very different from other Pharisaic preachers, except that he was somewhat extreme in the emphasis that he gave to the ethical, rather than the ritual, aspects of Judaism.

Jesus' career did not last long; perhaps one year, perhaps a little longer. As an observant Jew, he went to Jerusalem on a Passover pilgrimage. Since many Jews were assembled there during the holy days, the Romans were particularly alert for signs of rebellion at that time.

When either he or his followers asserted publicly that Jesus was the Messiah, the Romans took note. They knew that the Jews believed the Messiah would be a king, a descendant of the House of David who would sit on the throne of his ancestors to reign over an era of peace and well-being for all mankind. The Romans considered any potential Messiah as an intolerable affront to their Emperor. Pontius Pilate ordered that Jesus be nailed to a cross, the Roman form of execution for political offenders.

The rest of the story is not historical; it is based on faith. Those who loved Jesus could not accept the fact of his death. They claimed that he rose from the grave. Some of them insisted that they had seen him. They formed their own synagogue that differed from others only in the fact that its members awaited his imminent return. Their strong faith attracted others. Most of the newcomers were Palestinian Jews at first, but their numbers increased as more Hellenized Jews and Gentiles joined their ranks.

They were people who believed deeply that Jesus was more than a good Jew killed unjustly for a political offense. They believed that he could and would return and save them. As their numbers grew, they developed new ideas strongly influenced by the Hellenistic worldview. Their theology evolved as a cross-fertilization of Palestinian Judaism with Greek ideas about gods and goddesses, death and the afterlife. They blended Jewish and Greek rituals. Some elements of each culture were retained; they gradually developed a new religion, still rooted in Judaism but no longer part of it.

One of the most important new members of this sect (they called themselves Nazarenes) was the brilliant aristocratic Jew, Saul of Tarsus. As a young man, he had violently opposed the Nazarenes. About twenty years after the crucifixion (about 50

C.E.), however, he had an overwhelming vision while traveling to Damascus, which led him to accept the teachings of the new sect.

Saul was soon recognized as a charismatic and gifted leader of the new sect. He changed his name to Paul, and traveled widely throughout Asia Minor to convert people to his belief in Jesus as the Messiah. He established congregations of believers, and brought them together as the foundation of the Christian Church. Though Jesus was the object of Christian veneration, it was Paul, with his organizational genius, who founded Christianity.

As Paul traveled and wrote letters to those whom he had organized, he developed his thinking further. To be sure, he considered himself a Jew and believed that the new faith was the authentic continuation of Judaism. He introduced elements that are alien to Jewish thinking, however, and eliminated basic aspects of Jewish tradition. For example, he declared ritual circumcision to be no longer necessary. He argued that the Law of Moses had been superseded by the new Gospel based on faith in Jesus as the Messiah—or, to use the Greek word, *Christos* ("Christ"). He insisted that Gentiles do not have to convert to Judaism before being accepted as Nazarenes; faith in Jesus was sufficient. As more people entered the ranks, they brought with them the Hellenistic culture which was part of their world, and felt increasingly alienated from the Jews. By the time the Jewish people rebelled against Rome in 67, the early Christians no longer felt involved in the Jewish national struggle. They soon formed their own distinctive community.

As the Church developed, it moved farther away from the Synagogue. Some Christians sought to impress the Romans who ruled Palestine so harshly that they were not Jews, hoping thereby to be granted more privileges and to be exempt from religious persecution. These early Christians expressed anti-Jewish sentiments; their writings cast Jews in the role of villains. By the second century, the daughter quite definitely had moved out of the mother's home.

*Theological Differences*

The difference between Judaism and Christianity is much more complicated than simply the rejection or the acceptance of Jesus as the Messiah. To be sure, Jews could not accept him as Savior. He had not brought to fruition for them any of the promises that the Messiah was expected to fulfill. Christians, on the other hand, so modified the Jewish concept that it took on a different meaning. To Jews, the Messiah was to be a specially gifted human being who was created "in the image of God" like all other people. He would be wise, compassionate and able, a descendant of King David who would occupy the Judean throne. He would restore the sovereignty of the Jewish people and put an end to their exile. Moreover, he would bring physical and spiritual well-being to all nations, not only to the people Israel, ushering in a universal era of peace, harmony, and blessing for Jews and all mankind. The various peoples of the world would come to acknowledge and serve the one true God. No longer would they engage in war. They would live together amicably and justly. Jews never imagined the Messiah as a divinity. For them, the idea of God becoming man, or of man becoming divine, was a pagan belief.

Christianity radically altered the Jewish concept of the Messiah. Their Christ was not human like other mortals; he was part of the Godhead. Christians believed he had been sent to earth in human form not to redeem Israel and, through Israel, everyone else, but to save all humanity. His death on the cross was to serve this purpose.

Judaism and Christianity differ in their concepts of sin. Judaism views mankind as prone to commit sinful acts, but not as inherently sinful. If we do commit a sin, we can atone for it through repentance *(teshuvah)*. The process of repentance involves recognizing the transgression, confessing it, and deciding not to repeat it. The function of the Day of Atonement (Yom

Kippur) is to highlight both our need and our ability to effect our own atonement.

In classic Christianity, sin is a condition in which one is born. Baptism removes the original sin, but it does not remove future sins of people who are sinful by nature and who can be saved only by a change in their nature. That change cannot take place without help, however. Jesus is the source of that help. His death on the cross was a vicarious atonement for all sinful people, past and future. Only faith in Jesus makes salvation possible.

In Judaism, the responsibility for improving life and attaining goodness rests upon the individual. In Christianity, the individual is helpless without the Christ. In Judaism, there can be no intermediary between God and people; each individual must confront the Creator directly. In classic Christianity, Jesus is the intermediary. (And there are other intermediaries as well, such as priests, who are thought to be the direct successors of the Apostles.)

Judaism makes no dichotomy between flesh and spirit. It regards both as good, since both come from the Creator. It follows that sex is viewed as an expression of love channeled through marriage, not as a base animal instinct. Eating gives us an opportunity to strengthen the body; it is not just a biological necessity. Poverty is not esteemed as a means to greater piety, but is viewed as an unfortunate fact that must be remedied.

Historical Christianity, on the other hand, contrasts impurity of the flesh to purity of the soul. The soul should free itself from the physical as much as possible. Virginity, celibacy, and poverty are highly desirable states. Christian saints were those who succeeded in freeing themselves from physical desires and worldly concerns. The most righteous Jews, on the other hand, were recognized as having channeled their physical natures into ways of actively improving human conditions caused by the ills of society.

Both Judaism and Christianity insist upon monotheism. But

Jewish faith rests upon the uncompromising oneness and uniqueness of God. Christianity teaches the doctrine of the Trinity, of the one God consisting of three elements or aspects. Judaism believes that no power exists independent of God; neither Satan nor any supernatural being constitutes an independent force that can oppose or defy God. In contrast, historical Christianity and some present-day denominations believe in Satan as the power of evil which functions independently of God.

The two religions differ in their appraisal of miracles. In Judaism, miracles play a secondary role. The postbiblical rabbis often endeavored to provide rational explanations for miracles recorded in Scripture. Were all stories of miracles completely removed, Judaism would not be altered in any way. Christianity, on the other hand, assigns them prominence. Much is made of the miracles ascribed to Jesus. Miracles were also ascribed to many saints. Any attempt to eliminate miracles in Christianity would radically alter the very nature of its historical tradition.

Judaism assumes faith in God, and then leaves it to the individual. No assembly of religious authorities can vote to declare what may or may not be believed. What has been central to the Jewish tradition is correct conduct. Proper *behavior,* ritual and moral, is the most essential element. If people truly believe in a God of love and righteousness, it will be reflected in their behavior. Christianity stresses correct *belief.* It insists that one can be saved by faith. Authoritative bodies have met to formulate specific articles of belief. Judaism, of course, has also been concerned with faith, as Christianity has been concerned with deeds, but they have differed in their emphases.

Thus, although both religions accept the Hebrew Scriptures as sacred, and although they share the moral imperatives flowing from faith in one God, they differ in many fundamental conceptions of humanity and in many outlooks on life. These differences need not imply hostility or competition. They indicate two different approaches to the same goal, that of making God truly sovereign in the world. Each should attempt to understand the other without seeking to lure the adherents of one into the camp of the other. Both Jews and Christians need to live in conformity with the holiest teachings of their respective faiths, while demonstrating in thought and in deed what they hold in common. If they do, they will be testifying to the strength of their convictions and to the validity of their faiths.

## Suggested Readings for Further Study

Sandmel, Samuel, *The Genius of Paul* (New York: Farrar, Straus and Cudahy, 1958)

———, *We Jews and Jesus* (London and New York: Oxford University Press, 1965)

Weiss-Rosmarin, Trude, *Judaism and Christianity: The Differences* (New York: Jonathan David, 1965)

ADDITIONAL SUGGESTIONS

Bokser, Ben Zion, *Judaism and the Christian Tradition* (New York: Burning Bush Press, 1967)

Gordis, Robert, *Judaism in a Christian World* (New York: McGraw Hill, 1966)

Greenstone, Julius H., *The Messiah Idea in Jewish History* (Philadelphia: The Jewish Publication Society, 1943)

Littel, Franklin H., *The Crucifixion of the Jews* (New York: Harper and Row, 1975)

Samuel, Maurice, *You Gentiles* (New York: Harcourt, Brace and Company, 1924)

Schoeps, Hans Joachim, *The Jewish-Christian Argument* (London: Faber and Faber, 1963)

Silver, Abba Hillel, *Where Judaism Differs* (New York: MacMillan Company, 1956)

———, *A History of Messianic Speculations in Israel* (Boston: Beacon Press, 1959)

# CHAPTER 13

# A Personal Story of Conversion

RACHEL COWAN

*G*ROWING up in Wellesley, Massachusetts, a wealthy suburban community populated largely by white Protestants, I always assumed that I would raise my own children in a New England colonial house such as my ancestors had built. It would be on the side of a hill, shaded by leafy maples and apple trees in the summer, and surrounded by brilliant foliage in the fall. At Christmas we would cut our own tree, bake cookies, and put two candles in each window.

Today I am raising my children in a tenth-floor apartment on the Upper West Side of Manhattan. My husband and I have furnished it comfortably and eclectically. Prominent on our walls are paintings with Jewish themes; our bookcases house many volumes of books on Jewish subjects. Every Friday night we light Shabbat candles and recite *berakhot* over wine and *ḥallah* before dinner. At Ḥanukkah, each of the four of us lights his own *menorah*. On the last night, thirty-two candles shine out toward the neighbors in the building across the street.

My path to Judaism has taken me far from that New England hillside, but has brought me the sense of history and the feeling for place that I longed for as a child, and much more. It took me many years to decide to convert, but now I feel deeply rooted in Judaism. History, tradition, and a growing faith in God have given more meaning to my life than I ever imagined I would find.

Looking back at the lengthy process of conversion, I see several stages of development. As a child I was deeply influenced by my parents' humanism. They taught me early that one of my responsibilities in life is to fight prejudice and discrimination. They gave me *The Diary of Anne Frank* to read, and I always felt that she was a friend to whose memory I had to be loyal. I often felt I was defending her when I argued against the ignorant anti-Semitic ideas of my classmates. I knew no Jews in Wellesley, for there was a restrictive covenant preventing the sale of houses to them, but I had Jewish friends at summer camp and at college. They never discussed religion, however, so I knew very little about Judaism. Nevertheless, when I fell in love with Paul Cowan, I liked the fact that he was Jewish. I hoped he would be able to teach me something about Jewish traditions. He, however, had grown up in such an assimilated Jewish family that he knew nothing about any Jewish holidays.

My family attended the Unitarian Church in Wellesley, where I was active in the youth group and taught Sunday School. I agreed with the liberal ideas that the minister preached, and I loved the music and the beauty of the Christmas and Easter services. Once I met Paul, though, I thought it would be preferable to raise our children as Jews rather than as Unitarians, for they would have such a magnificent history to feel part of and such a rich culture to participate in. I also felt responsible to help maintain the chain of Jewish generations whose links had never been broken.

But it never occurred to me to convert when I married Paul. He barely knew any more about Judaism than I did, and it seemed unfair to expect *me* to convert if *he* didn't have to. Besides, nobody raised the issue with us. I knew I wanted to know more about Judaism, but that seemed like a project for us both to work on together.

If we were going to raise our children as Jews, we needed to learn many things. We didn't even know how to light a Ḥanukkah *menorah*. We asked friends to lead a Passover *Seder* for us, and to teach us how to light candles on Friday night. With a group of parents we started a weekly after-school Jewish learning center for the kids (the *Ḥavurah* School). Working on the curriculum with the teachers, we learned a great deal.

During those years I saw myself as a fellow-traveler. I felt that our family life was enriched and strengthened by the rituals we were beginning to incorporate into our life. I was proud of what our children were learning, and glad that Paul was coming to understand more about what being Jewish means, and what it meant to him. I enjoyed the things we were doing and felt lucky to be able to participate, but I never thought I would become Jewish. It was clear to me that one was Jewish either by virtue of birth and a shared cultural history, or because of a religious commitment. But no matter how good my *latkes, ḥallah,* or *gefilte* fish tasted, I would never have Jewish genes, or know what it was like to grow up Jewish. Furthermore, I did not consider myself a religious person. Therefore a conversion, which implied to me the taking on of a new faith, seemed to be out of the question.

It was important to me that the Jewish community we lived in regarded me as an integral part. Once, on our honeymoon, Paul and I had traveled in Israel. We met with sharp criticism from Israelis who learned that I was not Jewish. That was the first time I had been the object of prejudice, and it hurt. It made us wary of getting close to any organized Jewish group.

Several years after we started the *Ḥavurah* School, a group of parents and teachers began to meet once a month to read the Torah in English and to discuss what we read. We then began to enclose the discussion in a very abbreviated worship service. Paul and I also began to attend High Holy Day services conducted by a group of young Jews in the neighborhood. They met in a very crowded apartment, and shared leadership of the service. For several years I barely understood what was happening, but I liked the spirit, the singing, and the English text for the meditations. I began to look forward to *Rosh Hashanah,* and joined with Paul in fasting on *Yom Kippur.*

Then a terribly sad thing happened to our family. Paul's parents were both killed in a fire in their apartment. The horror and sadness of their death was made bearable for us by the *Havurah* community, who really took care of us. They brought us food, they took care of our children, they sat and talked with us. We had never heard of the Jewish tradition of mourning, sitting *shivah,* but they taught us what to do, and we found it comforting.

In the months after the fire, I found myself looking forward more eagerly to our worship services. In trying to make sense of my in-laws' lives and their deaths, I unexpectedly found myself struggling with questions of faith.

Over the next two years, I took several classes—one on the Book of Exodus, one on the Prophets, and one on Kabbalah. I discovered that Jewish study was fascinating. Our family visited Israel for six weeks. This time I felt at home there, and loved the country despite its many problems.

One day I realized that I felt very differently about converting. What had formerly seemed impossible now seemed totally natural. It was clear to me that Judaism would be the spiritual path I would follow, and that the Jewish community felt like home.

I still was troubled, however, by the question of what converting to Judaism implied about my relationship to my parents and siblings. I did not want to participate in a procedure which implied that my family background was not adequate, or that I had to reject who I was in order to become somebody new. Some Jewish texts are very negative about converts' origins, and I didn't want to do something that subscribed to that attitude. When I married Paul, a teacher of mine once said, I did not give up my past. Rather, I brought all my strengths to the new relationship. The same would be true of becoming Jewish. I would not be bringing Christian religious beliefs into my new faith, but I would bring to my new role as a Jew the strengths I had acquired as a person, many of them taught by my parents.

As Paul and I learned more and more about Judaism, we came to observe more Jewish practices. We stopped working on the Sabbath (Saturday), stopped going out on Friday nights, stopped eating the foods that were specifically forbidden in the Bible. For me, it was important to understand something about each new law before I observed it. I couldn't take them all on at once.

As I began to look for rabbis to supervise my conversion, I reaffirmed my belief that I could take on Jewish observance only gradually. I finally realized that I felt most comfortable as a Conservative Jew, not as an Orthodox one. The attitude to women in Orthodox Judaism was also an important factor, because I had learned about Judaism from people who believed that women should participate equally in all aspects of the service, and I valued that practice highly.

It was emotionally difficult for me to meet with many rabbis, trying to find those who would accept my decision and agree to serve on a *bet din* to supervise my conversion. It was both puzzling and painful to have to knock on so many doors, only to be told that my understanding of being Jewish was not appropriate for their standards. When I finally decided that I would have a Conservative conversion, a close friend who is a rabbi found two other rabbis who readily agreed to participate in the *bet din*.

The idea of the *mikvah* made me feel anxious. For one thing, I associated it with baptism, an idea I had always resisted. Of course I soon realized that baptism was derived from the *mikvah*, not *vice versa*, but I still felt that it would feel awkward to have to immerse myself in this strange bath under the supervision of an unknown (and, I assumed, probably judgmental) "*mikvah* lady." I asked my closest friend to come with me, as a witness who represented that part of the Jewish community with which I felt most closely identified.

The *mikvah* turned out to be a very clean, white-tiled, small pool. The "*mikvah* lady" was friendly and helpful. The water was warm and embracing, supporting, not strange. The lady made me dip twice to make sure that not even one hair went unimmersed. Then I repeated the blessings out loud so that the rabbis, who were standing outside the door, could hear.

I did not feel born again, nor did I feel cleansed. But I did feel that I had done something important, that it had helped me reach a new level in a spiritual journey that would last the rest of my life. As time passes, I appreciate the *mikvah* even more. It marked an important transition.

Rabbi Wolfe Kelman, who supervised my conversion, suggested that I invite my friends and family to an evening service at our synagogue in which I would participate. It was a wonderful idea because I could immediately do something significant to begin my life as a Jew. I had learned a passage from *K'riat Sh'ma,* which I led, and I learned to read one of the evening prayers. I also gave a short talk about my conversion. I wanted my mother and sister to hear that my decision grew out of my love for them, and I wanted my friends to understand more about my decision.

> To me, this is a very important moment, a moment of passage, but one that is part of a continuum. I used to think that conversion meant that you stopped being one thing in order to become something different, and for that reason I resisted it. But Adin Steinsaltz gave me a more organic metaphor. Conversion, he said, is like marriage. You are joined to a new community, but you bring to the union the strength and values that have been your foundation throughout your life. My conversion, for me, marks officially a love that I've already experienced deeply.

> That love began as the respect which my parents taught me for Jewish people, as the commitment which they instilled in me to

speak out against racisim and anti-Semitism. My sisters, Connie and Peggy, and my brother Richard, have always shared that commitment. I was moved last year when my mother asked Paul and me for books to read about Israel for, she said, "I have Jewish grandchildren, and they need a country where they'll always be safe."

I fell in love with Paul seventeen years ago. Over time I have felt my identification with the Jewish people broaden from him to his parents Polly and Lou, his brother Geoff and his sisters Holly and Liza, to my friends here tonight, to the larger community and the country Israel. It became increasingly important to me not simply to identify with Judaism, but to become a Jew. I've always been proud to be a Yankee from New England. Now I'm proud to be a Jew as well.

Finally, I'd like to talk about two of my most important teachers, Lisa and Matthew. Of course Paul and I have tried to influence their values and beliefs by sharing with them our ideas, our family histories—Midwestern Jewish and New England Protestant—and by creating places for them to learn: the Purple Circle Day Care and the *Ḥavurah* School. Our families and friends have also shared much with them. But we have also learned from them. They have shown us what they see as right and wrong, fair and unfair, important and trivial. I respect their opinions enormously.

Today marks an important step for me, a step in the search we all share to lead lives that are meaningful to ourselves and useful to others. I feel strengthened in that search by my children, my husband, my parents and siblings, and by my friends. I also feel strengthened by affirming publicly that an important part of the person I strive to be is being a Jew.

After the service, everyone came over to the house for a potluck supper. I made sure to include my non-Jewish friends, and my many Jewish friends who didn't think conversion was necessary for me to be a part of their lives, as well as my religious Jewish friends who were very happy that I had chosen to become Jewish.

It took a while after I officially became Jewish to feel Jewish. People in our synagogue were extremely accepting of me. I actually began to work there as program director a few months after my conversion. But just as born Jews often have difficulties in defining what being Jewish means to them, I, too, had a lot of growing to do. For a long time, I had been aware of not being Jewish. Now when people made remarks that I didn't look Jewish it took months until I was comfortable in saying to them that many Jews look different these days. When people referred casually to *shiksas* or to *goyim,* or said that a Jew by choice isn't really Jewish, I was not comfortable at first in pointing out the prejudice or insensitivity beneath such remarks.

Gradually my Jewish identity has grown stronger and stronger. On the first anniversary of my conversion, Paul bought me a corsage. Now I have trouble remembering how many years I have been Jewish because it seems like always. And this year, for the first time, I felt no loneliness at Christmas. We go every year to visit my sister for the holiday and each year I had felt a little sad that my kids don't "own" that holiday the way I did, and I felt a sense of separation from my sister. This year, though, I felt totally at peace with my decision. It was wonderful to be with her and her family, to share in their joy, but to realize that I had found other riches.

I have found a way of life that incorporates daily, weekly, and yearly observances, that has its own rich cycle, that meets my needs for tradition, for ceremony, for community, and for God. As I grow as a Jew, I also grow as a person. What separates me as a Jew makes me a stronger, more caring, patient person, better able to work with all kinds of people, and to work with them to make a world that is better for all of us.

# Closing Words

THIS book has sought to introduce you to a vast and sometimes complex subject: Judaism. Each topic dealt with deserves book-length treatment. (Some topics require several books!) I have restrained myself from expanding and elaborating because I did not want this introduction to be unwieldy. There is more to Judaism and Jewish life than can be covered in one book.

There are some subjects that I have omitted. One such subject is literature. I would have loved to include poems and excerpts from fiction and essays, stories, novels. I also had to forgo a presentation of Hebrew, Yiddish, Ladino, and other tongues dear to and developed by Jews. I deeply regret being unable to present a discussion of some contemporary issues in light of Jewish tradition.

Unfortunately, there are many Jews who do not know much about the subjects presented in this book. They may have memories of pious parents and grandparents; they may have attended a religious school in their preteen years or even until confirmation; they may have been members of a Jewish youth group. But the knowledge, which was neither extensive nor intensive when first acquired, faded as the years passed. As a result, converts often know more and observe more than those who were born into the Jewish people.

Such people have been in the back of my mind even while I was consciously addressing those in the process of becoming Jews. My personal goal has always been to persuade people to learn about Judaism, to convince Jews that they should make their decisions based upon Jewish tradition, to inform non-Jews that they will better understand their own religion and Western civilization if they learn the basic teachings of Judaism. Unfortunately, in high schools and universities, Western civilization is traced to its Greek and Roman roots but its Jewish roots are ignored.

There is no proselytizing note in this work. We Jews do not claim to possess the sole truth; we do not assert that non-Jews are mistaken or doomed or sinful. To be sure, we seek understanding and mutual respect. And those, we are convinced, require knowledge.

Whatever your reasons for wanting to understand the essentials of Judaism, we want to help you gain that comprehension and we hope that this volume has been helpful. A passage in the Mishnah discusses a number of practices for which there is no prescribed limit. They include respect for parents, acts of lovingkindness, and restoring peace between one person and another. This Mishnah concludes: *Vetalmud Torah k'neged kulam,* "the study of Torah is the most basic of them all." In a later generation, that conclusion was questioned. Why should "study of Torah" be more important than honoring father and mother, giving charity, and performing good deeds? The answer given: Through study, one learns what to do and how to act.

I hope that this book will lead you to understanding and that the understanding will lead you to good living, and, for those who are Jewish, to good *Jewish* living. If it accomplishes that, those of us engaged in presenting this work will be richly rewarded.

# Index

Abraham, 4, 5, 64, 103
*Adon Olam,* 47, 55
Afterlife, 15–17, 100–101
Aḥad Ha'am (Asher Ginzberg), 153
Akiba, Rabbi, 3, 87–88
*Aleinu,* 24, 45–46, 48, 49, 55
Alexander the Great, 108
*Aliyah,* 52–53, 68, 70, 93–94
*Amidah,* 22, 40–45, 48, 50, 54, 56, 70, 74
Andreas, bishop of Bari, 4
Antiochus, 71, 109
Anti-Semitism and repression, 5, 7, 72, 110
  in Europe, 117–120, 122–123, 125–127
  in the United States, 147–148, 175
  sources of, 130–134
Ark *(Aron Kodesh),* 51, 53, 59
*Ashrei,* 48
*Avodah,* 42
*Avot,* 41

*Baal korei,* 52, 53
Baal Shem Tov (Israel ben Eliezer), 123–124
*Barkhu,* 38, 56
*Bar mitzvah,* 11, 93–94
*Bat mitzvah,* 11, 93–94
Bene Israel, 136–137
*Berakhot* (blessings), 38–56, 64. *See also* Prayers; Synagogue services; *and individual blessings by name*
  after meals, 85
  before meals, 81–82, 84, 85, 174
  *brit milah,* 91
  candlelighting, 83–85, 176
  conversion, 8, 179
  marriage, 94–96
*Besamim,* 86
*Bet din,* 3, 7–8, 178
*Bimah,* 59, 60
*Birkat hamazon,* 85
*Birkhot Hashaḥar,* 47

Birth, 90–93
Blessings. *See Berakhot*
Blood Libel, 118
*Brit milah*. *See* Circumcision

Canaan, 103, 104
Candlelighting, 71–72, 83–85, 176
    blessing for, 83–85, 176
Cantor. *See Ḥazzan*
Charity. See Philanthropy; *Tzedakah*
Children, blessing of, 84–85
Chosen people, 4, 18–20
Christianity
    and Judaism, 3, 5, 6, 131–133, 147,
        148–149, 162–173
    conversion to, 28, 128
    tenets of faith, 6, 169, 170–173
Circumcision, 2, 9, 29, 90–93
Cochin, Jews of, 137
Confession, 66
Congregation, 55–60
Conservative Judaism, 7, 31–32, 33,
        34, 49, 55, 57, 62–63, 75–76,
        80–81, 96–97, 129, 144, 178
Conversion
    to Christianity, 28, 128
    to Judaism, ix–x, 1–10
        prohibition of, 3, 5
        ritual of, 2–3, 7–9, 178–181
Cyrus, 108

David (King), 21, 105–106
Death, 97–101
Divorce, 96–97
*Dreydl*, 72
Dreyfus, Alfred, 128, 153

Ecclesiastes, Book of, 68
Egypt, 68–69, 104, 158–159
*Ein Keloheinu*, 55
*El malei raḥamim*, 98
Emancipation, 27, 28, 127–130
*Erusin*, 94
Esther, Book of, 72
Eternal Light (*Ner Tamid*), 59

*Etrog*, 67–68
Exodus, 68–70, 104

Fasting, 65, 73, 85, 93
*Fleishig*, 80
Food and meals, 64, 67, 69, 71, 72, 73,
        78–81, 84, 85, 99. *See also*
        *Ḥametz; Kashrut*

*Gan eyden* (Garden of Eden), 16, 78
*Gaon, Geonim*, 114–115
Gaon of Vilna (Elijah of Vilna), 124
*Gehinnom* (Hell), 16–17
*Gemara*, 12, 113. *See also* Talmud
*Get*, 96–97
*Gevurot*, 41
God, 13–15, 103, 170–172
*Gollel*, 53
Gordis, Robert, 16, 17
*Grogger*, 72

*Haftarah*, 53, 54, 66, 70, 74, 93
*Haggadah*, 69–70, 82
*Halakhah*, x, 2–3, 6, 7–9, 12–13,
        19–25, 27–34, 91, 111–114
Halevi, Yehudah, 115–116
*Ḥallah*, 64, 84, 85, 174
*Hallel*, 67, 70, 74
*Ḥametz*, 69
*Hamotzi*, 64, 84, 85
Ḥanukkah, 21, 71–72, 109
*Ḥassidism*, 123–124
*Hatafat dam brit*, 9, 91
*Havdalah*, 66, 85
*Ḥazzan* (cantor), 57–58
Hebrew language, 7, 30, 31, 32, 37, 153,
        155
Helena, Queen of Adiabene, 2
Hellenism, 71, 108–109, 165–169
Herod, 110, 163
Herzl, Theodor, 153–154
Heschel, Abraham Joshua, x, 66,
        82–83, 86
*Ḥevrah kadishah*, 98
*Ḥibbat Tziyon*, 152–153

Hillel, *x*

Hirsch, Samson Raphael, 30

*Hodayah,* 42

*Ḥol ha-Mo'ed,* 67

Holy Days and Festivals, 62–73. *See
    also individual holy days by name*

*Hoshanot,* 67

Host, Desecration of the, 118

*Ḥuppah,* 94

Idolatry, 14–15

Isaiah, 22

Islam, 114, 123, 136

Israel (kingdom), 106–107

Israel, State of, 151–161

Jacobs, Louis, 13

Jesus, 162, 163, 167–168

Jonah, Book of, 66

Judah (kingdom), 106–108

Judah the Maccabee, 21, 71, 109

Judah, Rabbi ("The Prince"), 113

Judaism
    and Christianity, 3, 5, 6, 131–133,
        147, 148–149, 162–173
    and Islam, 114–117
    in Europe, 5, 27–31, 115–120,
        122–130, 133–134
        Eastern Europe, 31, 119–120,
            122–127, 145–147
        Enlightenment, 5, 27, 28, 127–130
        Holocaust, 126–127, 133–134
        Middle Ages, 5, 115
    in Israel, 159–160
    in the United States, 29–33,
        141–150
    modern movements, 27–34. *See also
        names of individual movements*

Judea, 108–111

*Kabbalat Shabbat,* 48–49

*Kaddish,* 46–47, 48, 56, 99, 100

Kaplan, Mordecai M., 32–33

*Kashrut,* 13, 20, 30, 32, 78–81

*Kedushah,* 42

*Keriah,* 98–99

*Ketubah,* 94–95, 97

*Kiddush,* 49, 64, 67, 84, 85

*Kol Nidre,* 65, 76

*K'riat Sh'ma,* 39–40, 48, 179

*Kvater, kvaterin,* 91

Lamentations, Book of, 73

*Lekha Dodi,* 49

Liturgy. *See Siddur*

*Lulav,* 67–68

Luria, Solomon, 5

*Maariv,* 38–47, 66

Maccabees, 109–110

*Maftir,* 53, 93

*Magbiah,* 53

*Magid,* 54

Maimonides, 4–5, 12, 14, 17, 47, 64,
    116–117, 135

Marriage, 1–2, 94–96
    and conversion, 1–2

*Matzah,* 69

*Megillah,* 72

Meir, Rabbi, 3

Mendelssohn, Moses, 128

*Menorah,* 60, 71–72. *See also*
    Candlelighting

Mercy, 24

Messiah, 24, 170

*Mezuzah,* 39–40, 77

*Mikvah,* 8–9, 178–179

*Milchig,* 80

Milk and meat, separation of, 79–80

*Minḥah,* 48

*Minyan,* 55, 56, 93, 99
    women counted in, 55

Mishnah, 12, 23, 113

*Mitnagdim,* 124

*Mitzvot,* 13, 19

*Mohel,* 9, 91

Monotheism, 13–15, 103, 171–172

Moses, *x,* 14, 88, 104

Mourning, 97–101

*Musaf,* 54–55

Music in synagogue, 28, 57–58, 59–60
Mysticism, 24, 49, 123

Names, Hebrew, 9, 91–92
*N'eelah,* 66
Neo-Orthodox Judaism, 30, 129
*Nesuin,* 95

Obadiah, 4
Oriental Jews, 134–138
Original Sin, 17
Orthodox Judaism, 7, 30–31, 33, 34,
      49, 55, 75–76, 80, 96–97,
      144–145, 160

Pale of Settlement, 125
*Parashah. See Sidrah*
*Paraveh,* 80
*Parokhet,* 51
Passover *(Pesaḥ),* 21, 66, 68–70, 100,
      176
Paul (Saul of Tarsus), 168–169
Peace *(shalom),* 21–22
*Pesaḥ. See* Passover
*Pesukei Dezimra,* 47
Pharisees, 164–166, 167
Philanthropy. *See also Tzedakah*
      in the United States, 143, 145, 147
      toward Israel, 160
*Pidyon haben,* 92
Pilgrimage Festivals, 66–71
Prayer, 3, 4, 13, 36–62. *See also
      Berakhot;* Synagogue services
Prayerbook. *See Siddur*
Prayer shawl. *See Tallit*
Prophets, 51, 105
Proselytizing, 1, 3–6
*Purim,* 72–73

Rabbinate, 7, 8, 11, 56–57, 95, 96–97,
      98
      women in, 57
Rashi (Rabbi Shlomo Yitzḥaki), 118
Rav, 16

Reconstructionist Judaism, 32–33, 34,
      57, 62
Reform Judaism, 7, 28–30, 33, 34, 49,
      55, 57, 62–63, 81, 128–129, 144
Repentance *(teshuvah),* 17–18, 43, 63,
      170
Revelation, *x*
Reward and Punishment, 15–17
Rome, 110–111, 163–168, 169
*Rosh Hashanah,* 18, 62–65
*Rosh Ḥodesh,* 54
Ruth, Book of, 71

Saadiah Gaon, 14, 114–115, 135
Sabbath, 29, 32, 48–50, 53, 54, 55,
      82–87, 174, 178
Sacrifice, 2–3, 54
Sadducees, 164–166
Samuel, Maurice, 132
Sanctity of life, 20–22, 78–79. *See also
      Kashrut*
*Sandek,* 91
Saul (King), 105
*Seder,* 21, 69–70
*Sefer Torah,* 50–54, 59, 68
Sephardic Judaism, 2–5, 134–138,
      141–143
Sermon, 28, 31, 54, 57
*Seudah shlishit,* 85
*Shabbat, Shabbos. See* Sabbath
*Shaḥarit,* 47–48, 50, 54
*Shamash,* 58
Shammai, *x*
*Shavuot,* 66, 68, 70–71, 100
Shabbatai Zevi, 123
*Shalom,* 43
*Sheva berakhot,* 95
*Shivah,* 99. *See also* Mourning
*Shloshim,* 99–100
*Sh'ma,* 13, 38–39
*Sh'mini Atzeret,* 68
*Shmoneh Esreh. See Amidah*
*Shofar,* 64, 66
*Shoḥet,* 79

*Shulḥan Arukh*, 31, 75–89
*Siddur*, 29, 30, 31, 32, 33, 34, 36–60.
    *See also* Berakhot; Prayer
*Sidrah*, 51–53
*Simḥat Torah*, 68
Sin, 15, 17–18, 66, 171
Solomon (King), 106
Song of Songs, 70
Study, 16, 23, 87–89, 124
  for conversion, 7
*Sukkah*, 66–67
*Sukkot*, 66–68, 100
Synagogue, 58–60
Synagogue services, 9, 11, 12, 28–33
  daily prayer, 36–48
  Ḥanukkah, 71
  in Conservative Judaism, 32
  in Orthodox Judaism, 30–31
  in Reconstructionist Judaism, 33
  in Reform Judaism, 28–30, 47
  music, 28, 57–58, 59–60
  Passover, 70
  Purim, 72
  Sabbath, 48–55, 60
  *Shavuot*, 70
  *Sukkot*, 66–67
  *Tisha B'Av*, 73
  *Yom Kippur*, 65–66

*Tallit*, 30, 40, 53, 76
  wearing of by women, 77
Talmud, 3, 87, 111–114
*Taref*, 79
*Tashlikh*, 65
*Tefillin*, 30, 76, 77
  wearing of by women, 77
Temple of Jerusalem, 42, 45, 54, 66,
    70, 71, 73, 95, 106, 107
  Second Temple, 1, 2, 21, 108–111,
    165
*Tevilah* (ritual immersion), 3, 8–9,
    178–179

*Tikkun leil Shavuot*, 70
*Tisha B'Av*, 73, 76
Torah, *x*, 1, 18, 19, 38, 46, 47, 50–54,
    66, 78–79, 87–89, 102–103,
    164–167
  reading of, 50–54, 68, 70, 93–94
*Treif*, 79
*Tu Bishvat*, 73
*Tzedakah*, 20, 22–25
*Tzitzit*, 40, 76

United States, 29–33, 141–150

Vegetarianism, 80
Vicilinus of Mainz, 3

Women
  as rabbis, 57
  *bat mitzvah*, 11, 93–94
  birth of a daughter, 92–93
  counted in *minyan*, 55
  participation in services, 31, 55, 68,
    93–94, 178
  *pidyon habat*, 93
  receiving aliyot, 93
  wearing of *tallit*, 77
  wearing of *tefillin*, 77
Work, prohibition of on Sabbath, 86

*Yahrzeit*, 47, 65, 100
*Yarmulke*, 30
Yiddish language, 7, 146
*Yigdal*, 12, 14, 47
*Yizkor*, 68, 100
Yoḥanan ben Zakkai, 111
*Yom Ha-atzmaut*, 73–74
*Yom Ha-shoah*, 74
*Yom Kippur*, 18, 62–66, 68, 76, 100,
    170

Zionism and Jewish nationalism, 7,
    28, 29–32, 42, 73–74, 151–161

ABOUT THE AUTHOR

*Simcha Kling, ordained by the Jewish Theological Seminary of America, is rabbi of Congregation Adath Jeshurun in Louisville, Kentucky.*